China:
The Balance Sheet

CHINA:
The Balance Sheet

What the World Needs to Know Now
About the Emerging Superpower

C. FRED BERGSTEN
BATES GILL
NICHOLAS R. LARDY
DEREK MITCHELL

PublicAffairs

NEW YORK

First published in hardcover in 2006 in the United States by PublicAffairs™, a member of the Perseus Books Group. Published in paperback in 2007 by PublicAffairs™.

Library of Congress Cataloging-in-Publication Data
China : the balance sheet : what the world needs to know now about the emerging super-power / C. Fred Bergsten ... [et al.].
cm.
  ISBN-13: 978-1-58648-464-4
  ISBN-10: 1-58648-464-8
Includes index.
China–Politics and government–1976- 2. China–Economic policy–2000- 3. National security–China. I. Bergsten, C. Fred.
DS779.26.C47285 2006
951.06–dc22
2006043793

Paperback: ISBN-13: 978-1-58648-435-4; ISBN-10: 1-58648-435-4

10 9 8 7 6 5 4 3 2 1

Contents

List of Illustrations   vii

Preface   ix

1 Summary and Overview:
Meeting the China Challenge   1

2 China's Domestic Economy:
Continued Growth or Collapse?   18

3 China's Domestic Transformation:
Democratization or Disorder?   40

4 China in the World Economy:
Opportunity or Threat?   73

5 China's Foreign and Security Policy:
Partner or Rival?   118

6 Conclusion:
Toward a New United States–China Relationship   155

Notes   163

Authors   181

Organizations   185

Acknowledgements   189

Advisory Committee   191

Index   193

List of Illustrations

Figures

3.1 Change in China's Working Age Population
(Aged 15–59) by Decade   47
3.2 Percentage of the Elderly (Aged 60 & Over) in
China and the United States by Decade   48
3.3 Ratio of Working-Age Chinese (Aged 15–59) to
Elderly Chinese (Aged 60 & Over) by Decade   49
4.1 U.S. Merchandise Trade Deficit with China, 1985–2005   79
4.2 China's Global Trade and Current Account Positions,
1992–2005E   82
4.3 Applied Tariff Rates, China and Other Emerging
Markets, 2004   83
4.4 China's Import Tariff Revenue as a Percent of the
Value of Imports, 1978–2004   85
4.5 Imports as a Percent of GDP in China, 1978–2005   86
4.6 Share of U.S. Trade Deficit, by Region, 1985 and 2004   91
4.7 China's Research and Development Expenditures,
2000–2004   101

Tables

4.1 China's Global Trade in High Technology Products,
1980–2005   102
4.2 U.S. Bilateral High Technology Trade with China,
1990–2004   102
5.1 China's Oil Imports by Region   131
5.2 Competing Statistics on China's Military Expenditure,
2005   150

Preface

China's rise as a global economic and political power is one of the transformative events of our time, and one of the most important challenges facing U.S. foreign and economic policy now and for many years to come. It is critical for the United States, and the world as a whole, to have a clear understanding of "the China challenge" and a sound analysis of its likely evolution and impact. This is particularly true since China's rise presents a complex mix of potential opportunities and risks, and of strengths and vulnerabilities—factors which, if correctly assessed, can be managed in ways that protect and promote U.S. interests, but which, if misunderstood or misinterpreted, could lead America in harmful strategic directions.

Yet untangling the strands of contemporary China is no easy proposition. China is an exceedingly complex, and sometimes internally contradictory, society that is difficult for outsiders to decipher. Indeed, there is no single "China" any more than there is a single "United States of America"; sharply different views exist within that country on most topics as the leadership struggles with immense challenges both at home and as an emerging power on the world scene. Hence it is unusually complicated to discern where China is headed over time on even the most fundamental economic and security issues. At the same time, the unpredictability of developments in the United States and other countries—and of their attitudes toward China—further complicates attempts to assess the impact China's course will have on its relations with the rest of the world.

Many efforts to develop a comprehensive and balanced perspective on China are unfortunately clouded, and even distorted, by the lenses through which various observers interpret what they see. It is natural that most multinational companies will emphasize the positive business opportunities offered by China while most American labor unions will focus on the risk of losing jobs to Chinese workers. Some devotees of *realpolitik* will fear that China's size and growing military capabilities will produce a new strategic threat to the United States and its allies while other observers see a strong and more self-confident China as a likely force for stability in the region and the world. Some analysts of China's evolution since its reforms in 1978 emphasize the significant improvement in living standards and way of life for much of the population while others stress continued governmental oppression of basic human rights and authoritarian political control.

In an effort to provide a basis for sound and sensible judgments concerning China, the Center for Strategic and International Studies and the Peter G. Peterson Institute for International Economics have undertaken a three-year China Balance Sheet Project, of which this book is the initial product. Because we believe that constructive U.S. policies toward China must rest, first and foremost, on a firm factual and analytical footing, this study's primary purpose is to provide comprehensive, balanced, and accurate information on all key aspects of China's own development and its implications for other nations. In an era when policy makers and the public alike are flooded with bits and pieces of information about China, we hope this book will provide "one stop shopping" for readers who want to grasp, in a single place, both the basics and the complexities concerning this dynamic country and its relationship with the world.

CSIS and the Institute undertook this project in tandem because we concluded that in order to present a comprehensive, holistic view of China, it was essential to consider the key economic, political, and security issues together, and indeed, to link them throughout. Dr. Nicholas Lardy, senior fellow at the Peter G. Peterson Institute for International Economics, took primary responsibility for Chapter 2, on China's domestic economy, and Chapter 4 on China in the world economy. Dr. Bates Gill, holder of the Freeman Chair in China Studies at CSIS, took primary responsibility for Chapter 3 on China's domestic transformation. Derek Mitchell, senior fellow in the International Security Program at CSIS, authored Chapter 5 on China's foreign and security policy. Dr. Gill and Dr. C. Fred Bergsten, director of the Peter G. Peterson Institute for International Economics, jointly authored the summary and overview in Chapter 1 and the concluding Chapter 6, which integrate the various topics, with substantial input from Dr. Lardy and Mr. Mitchell. All these authors have published extensively on their areas of expertise, as described in their biographical notes.

Carola McGiffert, fellow in the International Security Program at CSIS, served as executive director of the China Balance Sheet Project, and, with Dr. J. Bradford Jensen, deputy director of the Institute, led our administrative support team. Invaluable research assistance was provided by Chietigj Bajpaee, Melissa Murphy, and Xiaoqing Lu at CSIS and Giwon Jeong at the Institute.

We have been enormously assisted in the preparation of the book by an Advisory Committee of high-level experts on China and U.S.-China relations. The full committee has met with us on two occasions, at the outset of the project and to review a penultimate draft of the entire manuscript. Some of its members have also met separately with the authors of individual chapters for more in-depth consultation on particular sets of issues. We deeply appreciate the very important contributions of this group and look forward to working closely with them as the overall project continues. Our gratitude extends particularly to Ben W. Heineman, Jr., senior fellow at the Belfer Center for Science and International Affairs at Harvard University's John F. Kennedy School of Government, member of the CSIS Board of Trustees, and former senior vice president-general counsel of GE, who conceived of the project and helped it to reach this stage.

The findings and opinions in this book, however, rest with the four authors. They do not necessarily represent the views of our Advisory Committee members, contributing authors, and others who have provided support. A full list of Advisory Committee members, contributing authors, and other supporting individuals is at the end of this volume.

Over the next three years, we will continue to work together to bring thorough, objective information about China to light in an effort to help guide and frame a national discussion on China's rise and its significance. Follow-up activities will include conferences, around the country as well as in Washington, to discuss the findings of this book and the China challenge more broadly, and especially to develop further the policy implications of our analyses. We will also release more extensive papers on some of the issues addressed in the book, such as China's treatment of intellectual property rights and its agricultural policies, as well as conduct additional analyses of some of the most urgent and unsettled topics, such as the North Korea nuclear problem and China's currency policy. We plan to update, revise, and re-release the present volume in 2008 in an effort to maintain its accuracy and relevance. Our two institutions will also post a dedicated website—www. chinabalancesheet.org—to provide more extensive facts, figures, information, and analysis on China and U.S.-China relations.

The Center for Strategic and International Studies provides strategic insights and practical policy solutions to decision makers committed to advancing global security and prosperity. Founded in 1962, CSIS is a bipartisan, non-profit organization headquartered in Washington, DC, with more than 220 employees. CSIS's work is made possible thanks to the generous support of individuals, private foundations, U.S. and international government agencies, and corporations.

The Peter G. Peterson Institute for International Economics is a private, nonprofit institution for the study and discussion of international economic policy. Its purpose is to analyze important issues in that area and to develop and communicate practical new approaches for dealing with them. The Institute is completely nonpartisan. It is funded by a highly diversified group of philanthropic foundations, private corporations, and interested individuals.

Both institutions are financing the China Balance Sheet Project partially through their general institutional resources, which include support from the Freeman Foundation, William M. Keck, Jr. Foundation, and Starr Foundation. The project itself is partially underwritten by ACE Ltd, American International

Group, Boeing, Caterpillar, Citigroup, Coca-Cola, FedEx, General Electric, General Motors, Goldman Sachs, Microsoft, Pfizer, Procter & Gamble, and Tyco. These institutional supporters and underwriters had no editorial role in, or control over, the content of this book.

In an age when the United States is focused on many other critical challenges around the world, there may be no set of policies that matters more for our long-term interests than "getting China right." We hope that this book, and subsequent components of our China Balance Sheet Project, will make important contributions to this end.

John J. Hamre, President and CEO   *C. Fred Bergsten, Director*
Center for Strategic and   Peter G. Peterson Institute
International Studies   for International Economics

March 2006

China:
The Balance Sheet

1

Summary and Overview: Meeting the China Challenge

THE STAKES FOR GETTING CHINA POLICY RIGHT

Complex. Contradictory. Confusing. For centuries, China has proven difficult for Americans to understand. Today, however, China is becoming one of the most powerful countries in the world. As the twenty-first century unfurls, the stakes have never been higher for getting U.S. policy toward China right.

The direction that China and U.S.-China relations take will define the strategic future of the world for years to come. No relationship matters more—for better or for worse—in resolving the enduring challenges of our time: maintaining stability among great powers, sustaining global economic growth, stemming dangerous weapons proliferation, countering terrorism, and confronting new transnational threats of infectious disease, environmental degradation, international crime, and failing states. And for the United States in particular, a rising China has an increasingly important impact on American prosperity and security, calling for some clear-eyed thinking and tough economic, political, and security choices.

Put simply, the U.S.-China relationship is too big to disregard and too critical to misread.

Unfortunately, in spite of the unmistakable importance of the China challenge, there is often far more heat than light in the U.S. debate about China. Most worrying are the pessimism and alarmism that too often cloud the public's perspective, and which do not account for the enduring strengths and comparative advantages the United States can bring to bear in successfully meeting the challenge of a rising China.

To craft an intelligent, effective policy toward China, U.S. policy makers and the public alike need a serious, informed, and sustained assessment and debate on China's prospects and their implications for U.S. interests. This book offers a badly needed foundation for that discussion. Its principal aim is to provide comprehensive, authoritative, and accessible information and analysis on the increasingly complex economic, security, and political situation of China today, and its impact on the United States and the world.

ASKING THE RIGHT QUESTIONS

American strategy can—and must—respond to China's emergence in a way that assures regional security, realizes the greatest possible economic benefit, averts worst-case outcomes from China's socio-economic convulsions, and increasingly integrates the country as a partner—or at least not an active opponent—in achieving a prosperous and stable world order for future generations.

All this can be done—if the United States asks the right questions, understands China's complexities, and reinforces America's strengths.

Broadly speaking, the critical questions to be addressed fall into four basic categories:

- *Continued growth or collapse?* What are the real sources of China's spectacular economic growth? What are its most troubling economic weaknesses? Will China continue to grow at such a pace, or overheat and collapse in the next spectacular case of failed development and financial mismanagement?

- *Democratization or disorder?* Will further rapid economic growth in China inevitably lead to more pluralistic and even democratic forms of government? Will China's sociopolitical transformation lead to widespread upheaval and unrest? Or will the Chinese leadership maintain political control while orchestrating ever greater prosperity? What are the implications of these different outcomes for U.S. interests?

- *Economic opportunity or threat?* Does China represent a major threat to American jobs, living standards, and access to energy and other vital commodities? Do its large holdings of U.S. financial assets endanger U.S. stability? Or is China predominantly a beneficial driver of global economic prosperity, offering opportunities that outweigh the risks for businesses, workers, and consumers? What should the United States do to encourage the latter scenario?

- *Security partner or rival?* What are China's strategic intentions? Is China another pre-1914 or pre-1939 Germany? Imperial Japan? Soviet Russia? Something more troubling—or less so? Are China and the United States destined to become enemies? Or can Beijing and Washington, as they have in the past, realize a new strategic and mutually beneficial *modus vivendi*?

CHINA'S DOMESTIC ECONOMY: CONTINUED GROWTH OR COLLAPSE?

Chapter 2 addresses the first big set of questions with a close examination of China's domestic economic situation.

Many aspects of China's economic picture are impressive, even amazing. Already, China is the world's fourth largest economy and third largest trading nation. It has grown by about 10 percent per year for almost three decades, increasing its output by a factor of nine since launching its economic reforms in 1978. In the process, it has lifted more than 200 million people out of poverty.

Because China is so large and growing so rapidly, and also

because it is extremely open to the world economy, in recent years it has accounted for about 12 percent of all growth in world trade—much more than the United States. China has nearly become the world's largest surplus country; in 2006, its foreign exchange reserves will likely reach $1 trillion, far more than any other country's. China is second only to the United States as a recipient of foreign direct investment. It has used its deep and rapid integration into the world economy, which has left it with among the lowest trade barriers of any developing country, to overcome internal resistance to continuing economic reform. And at a time when the global economy is increasingly technology-driven, China is graduating hundreds of thousands of engineering and science students each year.

It is important, however, to also recognize the continuing weaknesses and downsides of China's domestic economy, especially in comparison to the United States. For example, despite its growth, China remains a poor country with per capita income averaging just one twenty-fifth that in America. China's average wage is one-thirtieth that of the United States and its average productivity level is equally lower (and wages, in any event, account for only 20 percent of the cost of producing textiles and 5 percent of the cost of producing semiconductors). China is seeking to advance to higher technology industries and greater value added, but it still spends only about 10 percent of what the United States devotes to research and development. Meanwhile, only about one-tenth of China's scientific graduates can compete internationally, and the great bulk of its "advanced technology" exports are commoditized products such as notebook computers, mobile phones, and DVD players.

Over the next few years, let alone over further decades, China faces daunting challenges to sustaining its breathtaking growth. These include completing the reform of state-owned enterprises; improving the allocation of capital, in part through cleaning up the banking system; developing new economic policy tools to promote stability; lessening the income gaps that have opened up between the urban and rural areas and the coastal and inland regions; coping with urbanization and labor reallocation on a scale unprecedented in history; and meeting its enormous needs for energy, other raw materials, food, and water in an environmentally sound way.

It is difficult to know how China's future development will affect its approach to the global economy and international security. It is also difficult to know whether China's continued economic success, even if sustained for another decade or more, will produce a more democratic polity that would presumably be more congenial to U.S. interests—though most countries that reach middle-income status do become far more open politically as well as economically.

Still, it is hardly inconceivable that China could seek to take advantage of becoming the world's largest economy, as may well happen, to revise the international trade and finance rules to its own advantage. It may seek to impose its will in other ways on both its nearby and distant neighbors. It may devote a sizeable share of its growing economy to military purposes, and thus pose at least a potential threat in ever-widening theaters of possible conflict.

Regarding China's domestic economy, Americans should understand that there are limits to what the United States can do. Only if China were to blatantly attack Taiwan, or belligerently threaten other neighbors in a manner that triggered a new Cold War, would Europe and, especially, Japan and other Asian countries even consider joining the United States in applying the far-reaching sanctions that would be necessary to have any chance of limiting China's economic advance. However, properly managed, U.S. policy can—and already does—shape China's international economic aims and security policy in a positive direction.

On the other hand, even without direct U.S. pressures, China will be hard-pressed to ensure continued epochal change in the economy with a political system frozen in time. The political system that existed in 1978 when annual income per capita was $200 had to adapt to manage the $1,700 per capita Chinese economy of today. The $10,000 per capita China of tomorrow will likewise require dramatically different governance. And Beijing knows it.

CHINA'S DOMESTIC TRANSFORMATION: DEMOCRATIZATION OR DISORDER?

Taking on the second big set of questions, Chapter 3 examines China's dynamic and sometimes convulsive domestic transformation and considers the prospects for significant political and social change.

The top priority for China's leadership is keeping a lid on the country's burgeoning political, economic, and social challenges—and thus keeping the Party in power. Yet China's leaders face a conundrum: They recognize the imperative of "*gaige kaifang*" ("reform and opening") so the Chinese people can compete, innovate, and prosper in a globalizing world, but they also know these transformative forces will fuel domestic change and upheaval.

Consider just a few of the complex challenges on China's domestic agenda. Some 140 million persons, or about 15 percent of China's workforce, are economic migrants on the move. China boasts some 300,000 U.S. dollar millionaires, but also has more than 400 million persons living on the equivalent of less than $2 a day. Only about 15 percent of China's land is arable, and that amount is shrinking.

Sixteen of the world's twenty most air-polluted cities are in China. More than three-quarters of the surface water flowing through China's urban areas is considered unsuitable for drinking or fishing, and 90 percent of urban groundwater is contaminated. The gap between China's rich and poor rivals that of the United States, and the gulf is growing wider. Social unrest is on the rise, from some 8,700 major incidents reported in 1993 to 87,000 "public order disturbances" reported in 2005.

China's public health and demographic indicators also point to troubles ahead. China is "graying" at a fast pace, and will grow "old" before it grows "rich." While China's life expectancy of just over 71 years is near developed-world levels, premature deaths from heart disease, stroke, and diabetes will result in a loss of more than half a *trillion* U.S. dollars over the next ten years. Seventy thousand new HIV infections occur in China every year.

The emergence of SARS, avian flu, tuberculosis, and other communicable diseases potentially threatens the health of millions of Chinese and millions more beyond China's borders.

But do all these problems add up to widespread chaos or significant political upheaval in the next five to ten years? For several important reasons, probably not. First, the Party leadership is intensely aware of these problems, and has become more adaptive: introducing piecemeal reforms, co-opting intellectual and business elites, imposing controls on information flows, and pronouncing policies aimed at alleviating the concerns of China's rural and urban poor.

Second, for the most part, the myriad challenges, while widespread, have not coalesced in a way that threatens either the political leadership or national stability. Currently, China's social unrest is highly localized, both geographically and in terms of specific grievances. On the other hand, when movements do appear to be well-organized and national in scope—such as the China Democracy Party or the Falun Gong—Beijing swiftly suppresses their activities.

Third, China continues to receive foreign technical assistance to help address its domestic challenges.

Finally, with China's foreign exchange reserves approaching $1 trillion in 2006, its leaders could bring considerable resources to bear on major problems if and as they choose.

Instead, it is more likely that the Chinese leadership will continue muddling through to deliver continued good economic prospects, maintain a hold on political power, and preserve basic order, despite a high incidence of unrest and growing socioeconomic ills.

But change is afoot. Today's China has over 390 million mobile phone subscribers, 111 million Internet users, 285,000 officially registered nongovernmental organizations, and some 140 million migrants on the move in search of economic opportunity. There are an estimated 70 million practicing Christians in China today—the equivalent of the total populations of Alabama, Florida, Kansas, Michigan, New York, Utah, Virginia, and Washington combined. Hundreds of millions of Chinese engage in traditional folk religions, worshipping local gods, heroes, and ancestors.

Meanwhile, though China is not a rule of law country, it now claims roughly 120,000 certified lawyers, 12,000 law firms, and more than 300 law schools—up from fewer than 2,000 lawyers and only two functioning law schools in 1979. China has incrementally improved the professionalism of its court system, strengthened procedural due process, opened up its legislative and regulatory processes, and introduced more consistent and predictable legal mechanisms, especially in administrative and economic law. While under single-party rule and far from a liberal democracy, Chinese society is more open today—economically, socially, and even politically—than it has been for the past half century or more.

Looking ahead over the near- to medium term, the United States should be prepared to deal with a China led by the Chinese Communist Party. This being the case, while calls for a more open, just, and democratic society in China must be an indispensable part of U.S. policy, they need to be tempered by informed and realistic expectations.

To begin, Americans should understand that Beijing's fixation on managing its domestic problems presents not only challenges but opportunities for the United States. It is true that Beijing's approach to managing its domestic challenges often translates into tight political controls on information and harsh crackdowns on dissent and unrest. On the other hand, with Chinese leaders focused predominantly inward, they are less inclined toward foreign adventurism. Moreover, China's real and growing domestic challenges offer enormous opportunities for the U.S. government and private sector to export ideas, expertise, and technologies, as well as the seeds for positive political, economic, and social development in China.

Doing what is possible to bring about positive outcomes in China clearly calls for intensified interaction by the U.S. public and private sectors with counterparts in China to address the country's domestic concerns. These activities will involve cooperation in a range of areas, including on energy and the environment, human rights, the rule of law, good government, anti-corruption, public health, social welfare, and the role of nongovernmental organizations.

The most compelling logic for such a course is that it is so clearly in the U.S. interest. An apprehensive, unstable, collapsing, or anarchic China could pose unacceptably high economic and security risks to the United States. Moreover, a weakening and wary China would probably also rein in the political and social progress of the past two decades. Even a relatively stable and growing China can spread problems across its borders, such as pollution, infectious diseases, organized crime, and trafficking in weapons, drugs, and people. Intensified interaction to help address China's domestic challenges would also improve the United States' ability to observe and accurately assess the country's circumstances and prospects going forward.

CHINA IN THE WORLD ECONOMY: OPPORTUNITY OR THREAT?

Chapter 4 looks at the next big set of key questions by presenting extensive data and analysis on China's international trade and economic activities.

Assuming current Chinese and U.S. growth rates continue, China will become the world's largest economy in thirty years. Its average income then would be about one-fourth of America's. China would also be by far the world's largest trading country. Its size alone would dominate Asia, and move it alongside the United States and the European Union as a global economic superpower. But it could also be the first economic superpower in history that is relatively poor in per capita income terms and guided by a non-democratic political system.

China's rise intensifies the pressures that technological change and globalization have already been bringing to bear for some time on less competitive portions of the American economy, and thus on domestic politics. In some low-skill and thus low-wage sectors, such as apparel and footwear, and in some low-technology industries that have become largely commoditized, such as color television sets, Chinese competition accelerates the decline already underway in U.S. domestic production and employment. Along with the growth of India and other rapidly developing countries, China's economic development places downward pressure on some U.S. wages and real incomes.

In addition, China's huge and rapidly growing bilateral trade surplus with the United States, which is far greater than Japan's ever reached in the past, generates strong U.S. political reactions. So will China's inevitable desire to buy major U.S. companies, as was seen in the emotional Congressional reaction to the China National Offshore Oil Company's bid for Unocal in 2005.

It is important, however, to place the impact of these changes in perspective. China is large enough and competitive enough to cause economic problems for the United States, but it has neither derailed our economy nor been the chief cause of our difficulties, any more than were Japan in the 1980s or other Asian countries in the early 1990s. All of these trends would be well underway with or without China. Indeed, China has seized much more of the U.S. market from other countries than from domestic U.S. production. None of China's gains have precluded the United States from achieving rapid economic growth, job creation, and indeed the attainment of virtually full employment, in the late 1990s and again today. Technology development and factors other than international competition have been much more important in limiting real wage gains and worsening U.S. income distribution in recent years.

China's adverse affects on the U.S. economy must also be set against the incontrovertible economic benefits China brings. Because of China's low-cost, high-quality products and its rapidly growing market for U.S. exports, the United States is on balance about $70 billion per year richer as a result of trade with China. China's exports to the United States and its investments in American financial assets help restrain U.S. inflation and interest rates, and thus permit faster economic growth and more job creation.

Different groups of Americans are affected differently by U.S. economic relations with China. Homeowners and workers in largely non-tradable industries, such as education and health care, which comprise much of the dominant services sector, benefit from lower product prices and interest rates. Low-wage apparel workers, though they gain relatively more than other Americans from the availability of low-cost Chinese products at Wal-Mart and elsewhere, may nevertheless be losers on balance as a result of the possible acceleration of their job dislocation. Companies that supply auto parts may lose market share to Chinese firms or to larger American companies that can source those products in China.

In response to the threats and opportunities China poses, the United States should pursue a three-part strategy. First, the United States must strive even more diligently to put its own house in order: correcting its budget and external imbalances; saving and investing more in its physical and especially human capital; strengthening its education system at both the K–12 level and at the high-skill end of the spectrum to produce a labor force that will be able to compete with China and others; and providing transitional assistance for those Americans adversely affected by the accelerated pace of change globalization has wrought.

There is no need for any new China-specific legislation in the United States, such as across-the-board tariffs, or for Executive Branch standards and regulations uniquely targeting China. But maintaining sound and successful economic policies overall, including energy policies, will be crucial—both to shore up U.S. self-confidence and to diminish the temptation to scapegoat foreigners, as occurred vis-à-vis Japan during the prolonged period of poor U.S. economic performance in the 1970s and 1980s.

Second, the United States must insist that China accept and implement the international norms that apply to the strongest economies—and which are thus most responsible for maintaining global prosperity and stability. (In so doing, the United States will have to acknowledge that China had little role in creating those norms and will presumably have views on them as it increasingly engages in the process.) This would include meeting World Trade Organization commitments, reducing remaining trade barriers, respecting intellectual property rights, reducing its large global current account surplus, and permitting a sizeable increase in the value of its currency. Chinese failure to play a cooperative international role will inevitably produce strong protectionist reactions against it in other parts of the world, including the United States.

Third, the United States—along with the growing list of other major economic powers—must increasingly engage China in the institutional management of the world economy. The global economic community should avoid a situation in which China exercises its influence to push for some regional economic and trading alternatives in lieu of greater participation in global economic initiatives and decision-making. China is leading the effort to create an Asian Monetary Facility that could become an alternative to the International Monetary Fund for regional purposes. It is working on a free trade agreement with its neighbors in Southeast Asia. Its strong support for and participation in the "10+3" summits—bringing together the ten nations of Southeast Asia with Japan, South Korea, and China—could evolve into a broader "East Asian Community," including a region-wide preferential trade zone that would discriminate against the United States.

Rather, the goal should be twofold: not only to encourage China to play by the rules, but also to mobilize its leadership talents in promoting globally desirable economic and political outcomes. The alternative to effective global integration of China will be increasing international frictions, both between the United States and China itself and between the United States and its other chief economic partners, notably Europe and Japan, as they differ over how to respond to the China challenge.

CHINA'S FOREIGN AND SECURITY POLICY: PARTNER OR RIVAL?

Chapter 5 examines China's foreign policy goals, its regional relationships, its military modernization efforts, and its perspective on the United States.

There is little evidence that China has developed and is pursuing a concrete and coherent long-term global strategy. Beijing's pattern of action suggests that its stated priorities—to "create a favorable international environment" to facilitate China's internal economic development, and to "preserve China's independence, sovereignty and territorial integrity"—indeed reflect the primary motivations behind China's current foreign and national security policy.

China's stated desire to develop its "comprehensive national power," whether economic, military, or otherwise, is connected to an ambition to achieve great power status, and to ensure that its interests and freedom of action are protected in international affairs. Its priority attention to domestic development has resulted in a posture today that seeks to set aside areas of disagreement in relations with other nations, promote economic ties, and reassure others about the peaceful nature of China's rise. Beijing has placed increasing emphasis on relations with its immediate periphery.

The search for natural resources, particularly energy, to fuel its economic growth has become an increasingly important component of Chinese foreign policy in recent years. This has led to reinvigorated relations with the developing world, where many of these resources are located, and often led to support for unsavory regimes such as Burma, Sudan, Zimbabwe, and Iran. China's goals of unification with Taiwan also serve as a central animating component of Chinese foreign policy, in particular to isolate the island internationally and prevent its permanent separation.

China places enormous value on maintaining a positive relationship with the United States, whose vast market remains critical to China's successful development and growth. Beijing thus has been very careful in recent years not to challenge Washington directly or aggressively on international issues vital to U.S. interests, such as Iraq. That said, China is ambivalent at best about the United States' military presence and political influence in East Asia. Chinese leaders may privately acknowledge that China has benefited from the regional peace and stability the U.S. presence offers, but Beijing remains deeply suspicious about longer-term

U.S. intentions toward China. From China's perspective, the U.S. military presence along its periphery, policy toward Taiwan, and promotion of democracy and human rights are potential threats.

Beijing calls openly for the creation of a "multi-polar world"— a thinly veiled challenge to U.S. "uni-polar" leadership. China has led in developing multilateral bodies in the region that exclude the United States, such as the Shanghai Cooperation Organization, the 10+3 process, and the East Asia Summit.

Yet there does not seem to be a coherent Chinese strategy to openly challenge U.S. global leadership or construct an anti-U.S. bloc. Instead, in recent years, China has adroitly taken advantage of American preoccupations elsewhere around the world to exploit weak spots in U.S. relationships and strengthen its own international ties, especially in Asia. While today the apparent purpose of China's outreach is largely defensive and focused on economic interests, this posture over time could form the basis for more assertive leadership to counterbalance the United States or oppose U.S interests more actively.

Since the early 1990s, and accelerating in recent years, China has set out to comprehensively modernize its military: in doctrine, training, education, force structure, and overall operational capability. Beijing has implemented double-digit increases to its defense budget nearly every year since 1991; placed a growing emphasis on air, maritime, and strategic missile capabilities; streamlined the People's Liberation Army to create a more professional, efficient fighting force; attempted to improve joint interoperability; and upgraded its weapons platforms, primarily through foreign acquisitions.

Beijing's doctrine, training, procurement, and deployment strategy in recent years seems to be motivated particularly to address a Taiwan scenario. China also has closely observed U.S. military operations over the past decade, and its assessment of evolving U.S. capabilities has also informed its military modernization decisions, most notably Beijing's recognition of the increasing importance of information technology in modern warfare.

Chinese leaders have no illusions that the People's Liberation

Army (PLA) is a match for the U.S. military. What China does seek are niche capabilities to exploit U.S. vulnerabilities in order to deter, complicate, and delay, if not defeat, U.S. (or other) intervention in a Taiwan scenario. Beijing also seeks more broadly to prevent the United States and its allies from containing China's economic and military development through military action or intimidation. While a Taiwan scenario may serve as a leading animating factor in China's military modernization strategy, operational capabilities developed in the process may have broader applications to assert Chinese territorial claims and other future interests beyond the Taiwan Strait.

There is little doubt that Beijing would take military action should it become clear that Taipei has foreclosed the possibility of future unification. However, at present, China seems to be taking a longer-term approach to the Taiwan question, to prevent independence rather than compel near-term unification. Such an approach is consistent with Beijing's focus on domestic development and on promoting a benign international image. It also reflects relative confidence in current trends in Taiwan politics, U.S. policy, and China's own military development to constrain Taiwan's options.

Longer-term trends are more troublesome, however. Even as cross-Strait economic ties continue to flourish, Taiwan national identity continues to grow, as will demands for greater international space. Meanwhile, China's deployment of missiles and other advanced military capabilities may create a decisive advantage for the mainland that could tempt Beijing toward a military solution or more aggressive attempts at coercion in the future. Populism and nationalism are also increasing on the mainland, which could put new pressure on the Chinese leadership to resolve the Taiwan issue. China's precise threshold for military action is unclear.

Looking ahead, nothing is preordained that the United States and China will become enemies. In fact, in political, economic, and national security terms, it is clearly in the interests of both sides to prevent such an outcome. China will need to increasingly recognize that as a rising power of 1.3 billion people, it cannot hide behind the notion that its impact on international affairs is minimal. Beijing will need to assume greater responsibility to act in ways that reinforce international norms above and beyond its immediate self-interest.

Washington will need to be prepared psychologically for the impact China's rise may have on the United States' relative power and influence in East Asia and beyond. While China is unlikely to challenge U.S. preeminence in political, economic, or military power for the foreseeable future, the rise in China's relative international power and influence may present economic challenges to the United States, and may alter U.S. strategic relationships with friends and even allies around the world as those nations accommodate China's rise.

The temptation for the United States to fall back on an actively hostile or antagonistic posture toward Beijing is a dangerous one for U.S. interests. Without serious provocation from Beijing, such a policy would isolate the United States and put Washington at odds with allies and friends around the world. The United States should remember that the international community is equally uncertain and concerned about the implications of China's rise for their interests, and will support, if sometimes only tacitly, reasonable U.S. moves to prevent the development of an irresponsible or dangerous China.

CONCLUSION: TOWARD A NEW UNITED STATES–CHINA RELATIONSHIP

China every day becomes all the more complex and contradictory. Gone is the bleak monolith of China's Maoist past. Today, in its place, there are many "Chinas"—rural and urban, wealthy and poor, educated and illiterate, international and isolated. Within this context of diversity and disparity, China's citizens and leadership are grappling with unprecedented domestic dynamism, coming to grips with globalization's challenges, and deliberating different political and economic futures.

U.S.-China relations are likewise complex and full of contradictions, all the more so as a result of deepening interdependence between the two powers. China stands as the United States' third largest trading partner and its second largest source of imports, shipping more than an eighth of what America buys from abroad. Sino-dollars get recycled to purchase American debt, helping finance the sizeable U.S. consumer and government spending deficits. Today, Chinese authorities are the second largest foreign official creditor to the United States, holding hundreds of billions of dollars of U.S financial assets. Meanwhile, the United States is China's number one bilateral trade partner and export destination, and an important source of investment, technology, and expertise. On the international political and foreign policy scene, U.S. and Chinese interests are also increasingly complex and interwoven, even as they also diverge on several key issues.

The revival of China in the late twentieth and early twenty-first centuries may turn out to be one of the greatest transformations in modern history, surpassing even the stunning rise of Japan from the 1960s forward, and the ascendancies of the United States, Germany, and the Soviet Union in the twentieth century. By virtue of its size and the possibility of its continued run of economic expansion, as well as the uniqueness of its economic and political systems for such a major economic actor, China poses challenges that are literally unprecedented.

In the face of these complexities, this book provides a foundation of information and analysis from which a well-informed debate and coherent strategy can emerge. Objective analysis of China can help Americans transcend love-it-or-fear-it simplicities that play out more colorfully in Washington as "panda huggers" versus "China hawks"—a false dichotomy that clouds a clear-eyed response to the China challenge.

2

China's Domestic Economy: Continued Growth or Collapse?

China has been the world's fastest growing economy for almost three decades, expanding at an average pace of almost 10 percent.[1] Real per capita output in 2005 was nine times that of 1978, when economic reform began. Real per capita output in Latin America, by comparison, increased only 10 percent over the same time period. Taking into account the recent upward revision in its 2004 output and preliminary estimates of GDP growth in 2005, China is now the world's fourth largest economy as measured in dollars at current exchange rates.[2]

Rapid economic growth has been accompanied by an improvement in most measures of well-being and a dramatic reduction in poverty. Life expectancy, already high by developing country standards at the outset of reforms, rose to 71 years by 2000, the date of China's last census. Adult illiteracy has been cut by two-thirds and now stands at only 7 percent. Through rapid growth and targeted government policies, China reduced the share of the rural population living below its official poverty line by nine-tenths, from more than 250 million in 1978 to only 26 million by 2004.[3]

Despite this impressive economic performance, China remains firmly in the ranks of the world's low-income economies.

In 2005, its per capita GDP was only $1,700—compared to $42,000 in the United States, a gap of twenty-five to one. While China's economy could eventually be larger than that of the United States, this prospect is a long way off—and even then, China's per capita income at that time would remain far less than America's. For example, if both countries continue to expand at their past decade's average rate of growth, China's economy would not exceed that of the United States until 2035.[4] However, based on UN medium variant population projections for both countries, per capita income in the United States would still be almost four times China's.[5] Nonetheless, taking just 30 years to reduce the per capita GDP gap from twenty-five to one to four to one would be an impressive accomplishment.

WHY HAS CHINA GROWN SO RAPIDLY?

Five key factors underlie China's stunning growth performance over the past three decades: the embrace of market forces, the opening of the economy to trade and inward direct investment, high levels of savings and investment, the structural transformation of the labor force, and investments in primary school education.

Prior to reform, bureaucrats in China's State Planning Commission were responsible for allocating key industrial commodities such as steel and machinery and the state rationed consumer goods ranging from basics such as grain and cotton cloth to bicycles and the few other consumer durables that were then available. The State Price Commission established the prices of most commodities somewhat arbitrarily so there was little connection between profits and productivity. Market forces came into play only in rural free markets where peasants sold food produced on their private plots.

Similarly, on the eve of reform, China lacked a market for labor. In urban areas the state assigned jobs to individuals when they finished their schooling, the structure of wages was set by the state, and there was little labor turnover. Moreover, stringent controls on the migration of labor from the countryside into urban areas meant that most rural labor was bottled up in relatively low productivity farming and small-scale rural industry.

The state also played a very large role in capital allocation. A quarter of all investment was financed through the state budget. Meanwhile, the state heavily influenced the flow of bank loans for investment purposes in a process that was euphemistically referred to as "policy lending." There were no stock or bond markets and the state rigidly controlled interest rates on bank deposits and loans.

Over the first two decades of economic reform, market forces gradually displaced these non-market institutional arrangements. The share of output allocated through the plan fell sharply and market-determined prices replaced those of the planning authorities for all but a handful of goods and services. In urban areas individuals now compete for jobs, wages are flexible, and labor turnover is considerable. Moreover, the state has eased rural-to-urban migration barriers, creating a more integrated labor market.

Progress toward market allocation of investment resources has been slower than for goods and labor, but important progress has been made. The role of the budget in financing investment has declined precipitously; banks are in transition to a commercial orientation in which loans are extended on the basis of expected returns rather than political guidance; and China's central bank, the People's Bank of China, significantly liberalized interest rates on loans in the fall of 2004. China created stock and corporate bond markets more than a decade ago, but they have fallen far short of expectations and still provide only a tiny share of investment funds in the economy.

Nonetheless, the reform of markets for goods has had a very positive indirect effect on capital allocation. This is because retained earnings of companies are the single largest source of investment funds and, in contrast to the early years of reform, today productivity and profitability are highly correlated. More efficient firms now have higher profitability and are able to expand more rapidly, while less efficient firms have lower profits and, on average, grow more slowly and in some cases even go bankrupt.

The second key factor driving economic growth over the past three decades has been increased openness to the global economy, leading to a marked change in market structure and more competition. As will be detailed in Chapter 4, trade liberalization measures introduced by China's leadership have made its economy one of the most open in the developing world. Not only is its trade share of GDP unusually high, about two-thirds in 2005, joint ventures and wholly foreign-owned companies produce about 30 percent of manufactured goods, a share half again as high as in the United States. About three-fifths of these goods are sold on the domestic market, rather than being exported.[6] As a result, domestic firms must compete not only with large volumes of imports, but also with large quantities of goods produced by foreign firms in China. Since these foreign firms have advantages such as technology, design, and marketing, they add substantially to domestic market competition. As China's leaders correctly anticipated, domestic firms have had to increase their efficiency to survive.

The third factor underlying China's rapid economic growth has been high levels of savings and investment. China's sustained rates of investment are much higher than other developing countries at comparable levels of per capita income. This has allowed an exceptionally rapid growth of the capital stock, which in turn has facilitated the transfer of labor from agriculture to the modern sector, thus contributing strongly to economic growth. A little more than a third of output was invested in the 1980s; this figure has risen even higher over the past decade. Although China has received large amounts of foreign direct investment, these funds in recent years have financed only about 5 percent of capital formation. Moreover, domestic savings have been more than sufficient to finance the high level of capital formation that has characterized the last three decades of economic growth. As a result, China has been a net supplier of capital to the rest of the world. Among other lower middle-income economies, only a handful of oil exporting countries are in a similar position.

The fourth factor underlying China's unusually strong growth performance has been the sectoral transformation of its labor force. The share of the labor force employed in agriculture has declined from 70 percent at the outset of reform to about 50 percent today. China's extreme shortage of arable land means that agricultural productivity is extremely low, as measured by output per worker—only about one-sixteenth the average in manufacturing and services.[7] Thus, as workers leave agriculture and are absorbed in either manufacturing or services, major productivity gains ensue.

Finally, China's investments in primary school education meant that on the eve of reform it had a relatively high literacy rate for a very low-income country; for example, China's adult literacy rate in 1977 was 66 percent, almost twice the 36 percent rate in India.[8] The government further enhanced the policy emphasis on mass literacy, which can be traced to the 1950s, by promulgating the 1986 Compulsory Education Law, which increased mandatory education from five years to nine. China also has been far more successful than India in holding down gender differences in literacy. By the mid-1990s, China's adult literacy rate was just over 80 percent, compared to just over 50 percent in India—but China's female literacy rate was 73 percent, compared to 38 percent in India.[9] This gave China a crucial advantage in attracting foreign investment in manufacturing. Much foreign manufacturing in China is assembly activity and the work force is disproportionately female and recruited largely from rural areas. Basic literacy has been a crucial prerequisite to the creation of a relatively productive work force in these foreign manufacturing establishments.

Over the next decade, each of these factors should continue to contribute positively to China's economic growth. China's WTO commitments are further enhancing the role of the market, particularly in financial, distribution, and other services—domains where the introduction of market forces had lagged compared to the goods and labor markets. China's WTO commitments have locked in and even added, at the margin, to the openness that had already existed prior to accession in 2001. High levels of household savings are likely to persist for another decade, but may fall thereafter as the population begins to age and the share of citizens in the dissaving retirement years rises. This, however, will be a gradual process, and if further essential reforms in the banking and financial system improve capital allocation, a fast pace of economic growth could be sustained with a somewhat lower investment rate. The structural transformation of the labor force, too, will remain an important contributor to economic growth, as the half of the labor force still in agriculture continues to shrink over the coming decades. Finally, China is likely to continue to emphasize the investments in education that have made a major contribution to rapid growth in the first decades of economic reform.

WHAT ARE THE MAJOR OBSTACLES TO SUSTAINING ECONOMIC GROWTH?

Even though all of the underlying economic fundamentals are likely to remain very positive over the next decade or so, China faces three critical economic challenges in sustaining growth. These are, first, to complete the reform of state-owned enterprises; second, to develop a more efficient capital allocation mechanism; and third, to develop macroeconomic policy instruments to moderate the fluctuations that have marked the high-growth era. Absent meaningful progress in these three areas, China may not be able to sustain its stellar pace of economic growth.

In this regard, it is useful to recall the lessons of economic history. Straight-line economic growth extrapolations are rarely warranted, particularly over long periods of time. In the 1980s, for example, Japan was frequently portrayed as a looming economic giant. But Japan's flawed economic policies led to more than a decade of economic stagnation starting in the early 1990s. As a result, the size of the Japanese economy relative to that of the United States and Japan's share of global trade both shrank dramatically.

China has made real progress in reforming its state-owned firms. Because of privatizations, mergers, and bankruptcy, the number of state-owned and state-controlled firms has dropped from 300,000 a decade ago to 150,000 today. At the same time, employment in these firms has been cut by 40 percent—about 45 million jobs. The decline was concentrated in the state-owned manufacturing sector, where 80 percent of employees—25 million people—have lost their jobs. Meanwhile, the productivity and profitability of most remaining state-owned firms have improved markedly.

There remain, however, a consequential minority of these firms that earn less than their cost of capital. Many of these actually have a negative return on assets, meaning that they would not be viable even if they were restructured in a bankruptcy that wiped out their debts. The majority of these firms are controlled by sub-national governments, which are reluctant to close them because workers would lose their jobs, potentially exacerbating social unrest. The financial cost of sustaining these firms, which is borne in part by local government budgets and in part by the banking system, is substantially less than a decade ago. But it diverts budgetary resources that would better go to pressing health and education needs. Equally important, it is obstructing full commercialization of the banking system.

A second fundamental challenge is developing a more efficient mechanism for allocating investment resources. The magnitude of the challenge is suggested by the rise over the past decade in the number of units of capital needed to produce one additional unit of output and the declining contribution of improvements in multifactor productivity to economic growth since the late 1990s.[10] These trends are presumably driven by China's investment rate, which has risen significantly over this period; by 2005 it had reached about 40 percent of GDP—higher than the peak investment ratios that prevailed in Japan, South Korea, and Taiwan at comparable periods of economic development. But China is growing no more rapidly than those countries did during their periods of high investment, suggesting that China's financial system allocates capital inefficiently. As Martin Wolf, the chief economics commentator for the *Financial Times*, observed, "What is remarkable is not how quickly China's economy has grown, but rather how slowly it has done so."[11]

Despite multifaceted efforts to address this issue, progress remains limited. China created a domestic stock market more than a decade ago, but it has yet to efficiently allocate investment funds to the corporate sector. Even prior to the virtual suspension of new stock listings in mid-2004, funds raised in recent years in the domestic equities market were the source of under 5 percent of all investment. Many Chinese securities firms are insolvent, and China has failed to develop a market driven listing process, institutional investors, and other arrangements necessary for a well-functioning stock market. The market for corporate debt is also modest, despite a decade of official lip service to its development.

Banks remain the predominant mechanism by which savings are intermediated to investment. Although the state has massively recapitalized three major state-owned banks, which now have strong balance sheets, the banks in general have made only modest progress toward operating on a commercial basis. They have high cost structures and limited risk assessment skills, and suffer from seemingly endless corruption. As a result, the earning power of the banks remains modest—especially for those that have not been recapitalized through government funds and must still provision for non-performing loans.

The willingness of China's leadership to sell minority stakes in its banks to strategic foreign investors is a promising sign. In 2005, for example, Bank of America spent $3 billion on a 10 percent ownership stake in the China Construction Bank (CCB).[12] Bank of America also entered into an exclusive agreement to provide CCB with strategic assistance in risk management, corporate governance, credit cards, consumer banking, global treasury services, and information technology. It is likely to be some years, however, before this strategy, which is also being pursued by Bank of China and the Industrial and Commercial Bank of China with other strategic foreign investors, yields major improvement in underlying bank performance.

Finally, even if the prospects for China's continued rapid expansion are favorable, it should be acknowledged that growth so far has been marked by considerable volatility. China's leadership faces a substantial challenge in developing more flexible monetary and fiscal policy instruments that could be used to mitigate the macroeconomic cycles that have characterized the reform era. Moreover, as China's integration into the global economy deepens, its vulnerability to external shocks rises. That underscores the desirability of developing independent monetary policy instruments to lessen such shocks—which in turn requires the adoption of a more flexible exchange rate regime.

These issues are best illuminated by a brief analysis of China's current macroeconomic challenges. Over the past few years China has become increasingly dependent on increases in investment to drive economic growth. Beginning in 2001, investment grew much more rapidly than GDP. As a result, by 2004 the share of investment in GDP had reached about 40 percent. The government, starting in mid-2003 and with greater vigor from mid-2004, took administrative measures to slow the flow of lending to sectors in which it anticipated the emergence of excess capacity. In 2005, as investment growth slowed, demand for imported machinery and equipment moderated, leading to a sharp increase in China's global trade surplus. Indeed, the increase in the trade surplus was so large that overall economic growth remained strong, despite the moderation in domestic demand.

As early as December 2004, at its annual Central Economic Work Conference, the Chinese Communist Party recognized the need to readjust the relationship between investment and consumption as sources of economic growth. This theme was reiterated and refined by the central bank in its mid-year 2005 monetary policy report.[13] In the bank's view, investment growth needed to slow further to allow demand to catch up with supply in sectors, such as steel, aluminum, cement, real estate, and even electric power, where excess capacity was evident or predictable. The bank also doubted the sustainability of the rapid growth of net exports evident in the first half of 2005, if for no other reason than the likely rise of foreign protectionism. The bank concluded that China needed to transition to a growth path that was more dependent on increasing consumption demand. This theme has since been reiterated in a number of important government documents, most notably in the Outline for the Eleventh Five-Year

Program, which was approved by the Central Committee of the Party in October 2005.

In many economies, governments can increase consumption through fiscal stimulus in the form of tax cuts on household income. This avenue is of limited relevance in China, where direct taxes on households are relatively small. In 2004, for example, combined government tax revenue from the personal income tax, levied on income of employees in the modern sector, and the agricultural tax, levied on peasant income, was only 1 percent of GDP. By comparison, the personal income tax in the United States prior to the major income tax cut under President George Bush in 2001 represented almost 10 percent of GDP. Thus, the Chinese government's announced plans for 2006, which include doubling the monthly income exemption from the personal income tax and eliminating the agricultural tax, are likely to have only a modest effect on household consumption.

The alternative form of fiscal expansion is expenditure-based. If tax cuts are insufficient to increase private consumption significantly, the government can increase its budgetary expenditures to add to domestic demand. Given already high levels of investment and the emergence of excess capacity in many industries, however, the government needs to increase its non-investment outlays, notably those on health, education, welfare, and pensions. There is enormous scope to do so, since governments at all levels combined in China spend only about 3.5 percent of GDP on these programs. In the short run, however, the situation may be less favorable. First, since the existing level of expenditure is so low, even dramatic proportional increases in these outlays would stimulate economic growth only modestly. Second, quantum jumps in such expenditures may not be technically feasible, at least in the short run. For example, increases in health expenditure are constrained by the paucity of trained medical staff, which can only be alleviated over time through increased training of doctors and other medical professionals.

Given China's government tax and expenditure structure, increases in private consumption expenditure will depend to an unusual degree on a reduction in the savings rate of households, which has been running at about 25 percent of disposable income since 2000.[14] By contrast in the United States in 2005 households spent more than their disposable income, i.e., the savings rate was slightly negative! But reducing the household savings rate in China is a formidable task given that motivation for household savings seems primarily precautionary. Only about one-seventh of the population, for example, is covered by basic health insurance, so many households save to cover future medical expenses.[15] Families also save for retirement because the basic pension scheme covers only about 16 percent of the economically active population—and in any case is designed to provide a pension equal to only 20 percent of average local wages, independent of a worker's lifetime earnings. Finally, households undertake a large share of expenditures on education, since government expenditures on education amount to only 2 percent of GDP.[16] Primary school fees are a large financial burden, particularly for poorer rural households.[17]

In the long run, of course, increased provision of health, education, and other social services through the government budget may reduce the precautionary demand for savings on the part of households. As families gain confidence that the government will provide more of these services, they may reduce their own savings voluntarily, i.e., increase consumption as a share of their own disposable income. Thus, the transition to a more consumption-driven growth path will probably need to start with increased government consumption expenditures, but with time is likely to be reinforced by changes in household consumption and savings decisions.

While it may take time, such a transition would be a welcome development for the United States and the global economy. As will be detailed in Chapter 4, China emerged in 2004–2005 as one of the largest global surplus countries—and thus has become, along with the United States, a major source of global economic imbalances.

Parallel actions by China and the United States, respectively the most important countries with unusually high and low savings rates, could make a major contribution to reducing these imbalances. If China's households reduce their savings rate,

China's current account surplus will decline. This adjustment should be facilitated by an appreciation of the Chinese currency, which would mitigate the inflationary pressures that otherwise might emerge as savings' share of income fell and the share of consumption rose. Meanwhile, there would need to be a simultaneous upward adjustment of the U.S. savings rate—either through a reduction of the federal government fiscal deficit or an increase in household savings. The latter would most likely result from a cooling of the housing market, which has fueled high consumption expenditures in recent years.

Mitigating short-term macroeconomic fluctuations in China also will require a more effective monetary policy. In recent years, the central bank has depended primarily on window guidance and other administrative measures to control the pace of lending from the banking system. Yet the use of these instruments undermines the goal of creating a commercially oriented banking system. The central bank needs greater authority to independently set benchmark interest rates; meanwhile, banks need to become more sensitive to rate changes.

Greater exchange rate flexibility would increase the scope for the central bank to pursue an independent monetary policy. Although the bank has had some success in sterilizing large inflows of foreign capital, it has occasionally been reluctant to raise domestic interest rates for fear that these inflows could become unmanageably large. Fixed domestic interest rates in 2003, when price inflation was rising, led to negative real interest rates that fueled a very large increase in bank lending and thus a sharp increase in capital formation. A more flexible exchange rate policy would have allowed greater flexibility of domestic interest rate policy and thus a potential mitigation of the cyclical character of investment.

WHAT OTHER MAJOR ECONOMIC CHALLENGES DOES CHINA FACE?

Beyond the three fundamental challenges discussed above, commentators point to a range of other economic factors that could derail China's economic growth. In some cases, these factors are misunderstood or exaggerated—but regardless, if China deals successfully with its three key challenges, its leadership will likely adopt policies and have the resources to address these other issues.

Growing Income Inequality

While economic reforms have brought unprecedented prosperity to China, income inequality has increased noticeably. When reform began, rural income inequality was remarkably low by international standards, largely because arable land was distributed relatively evenly among village households and non-farm income-earning opportunities were limited. In cities, the state imposed an extremely compressed wage structure, so urban income inequality was also low. It is true that severe restrictions on rural-to-urban migration had led to a huge gap between urban and rural incomes and living standards. Overall, however, in the late 1970s, China's inequality levels were among the world's lowest.

Twenty-five years later, inequality has increased greatly in all dimensions. In the countryside, expanded opportunities to earn income in periurban areas have led to rising income differences between those who live near cities and those in more remote rural areas. In urban areas the old state-controlled wage system has lapsed, with a resulting large and growing wage gap between those with higher levels of education and skills and those with more limited human capital endowments. The gap between the coast and inland areas also has risen as China's increasing participation in global trade has stimulated investment and provided increased job opportunities to those living in cities near major ports. Cities in remote interior regions suffer the disadvantage of higher transport costs, are less able to participate in China's booming export sector, and experience slower growth of employment and wages. Even the urban-rural income gap, already large at the outset of reform, has risen. Consequently, while China's overall level of income inequality does not yet match that of

Argentina, Brazil, or Chile, it significantly exceeds that of India, Bangladesh, and Indonesia.[18]

In the early 1980s, Deng Xiaoping dismissed the potential problems of growing inequality with the trenchant phrase "some people have to get rich first." China's current leaders are much less sanguine. Even though rapid economic growth has reduced the number of rural Chinese living below the official poverty line by 90 percent, the leadership believes that relative inequality has now increased so massively that it could threaten political stability. In response, they have prioritized policies to accelerate both the pace of farm income growth and economic development in lagging interior provinces.

In the short run, however, these policies are unlikely to reduce income inequality; on the contrary, income inequality could continue to rise for another decade. Other developing countries' experience suggests that income inequality typically rises in the early stages of economic development and starts falling when per capita income hits a level that China will not attain for at least a decade.

Despite rising income inequality, the real incomes of the poor have risen quite rapidly during the reform era. This is a case in which the rising tide has lifted all boats. If economic growth continues to be robust, the poorest elements of Chinese society are likely to see substantial further real income gains. If this is the case, it is unlikely that rising relative income inequality alone will become a major source of social unrest or a key impediment to sustaining rapid economic growth.

Rapid Urbanization, Unemployment, and a Changing Labor Market

On an absolute scale, China's current pace of urbanization is unparalleled in history. China's urban population has ballooned by an astounding 200 million over the last decade—the equivalent of two-thirds of the entire population of the United States. This has led to unprecedented increases in demand for urban housing, transportation, water and sewage systems, and other urban infrastructure. In 2005–2006 government expenditures for water supply systems in urban areas alone are expected to reach about $120 billion. Yet, even with these massive expenditures, fewer than half of China's cities currently provide any municipal sewage treatment.[19]

China is simultaneously struggling to provide employment for its rapidly growing urban population. This challenge stems from two sources. First, the combination of natural population increase and rural-to-urban migration results in continuous large additions to the urban labor supply. In addition, restructuring and downsizing of state-owned companies, mostly located in urban areas, has led to massive layoffs. As a result, even official numbers on unemployment, which only cover urban areas and measure only a fraction of those seeking work, soared to 8.4 million in 2005—a record level. Independent estimates by Chinese economists such as Hu Angang, using measures similar to those used in market economies, suggest that in recent years, China's urban unemployment rate has been 11 to 12 percent, almost three times the official rate. That implies that urban unemployment realistically measured may be in the range of 20–25 million.

While urbanization is a major challenge, it has also become a major source of economic growth. On the demand side of the equation, investment in property, including office buildings, commercial space, and private housing, has become and is likely to remain a major driver of economic growth. On the supply side, as already noted, the marginal worker in manufacturing and services is sixteen times more productive than an agricultural worker, so as migration proceeds, economic growth is boosted dramatically.

Of course, the pace of urbanization still needs to be controlled. Higher productivity to a considerable extent reflects more capital per worker in the modern sector. This capital accumulates over time, so there is a limit on the modern sector's ability to absorb a large share of under-employed agricultural workers in the short run. Because the regime has only partially liberalized controls on place of residence, to date it has been able to prevent the rise of massive urban slums that have characterized large parts of Latin America and South Asia in recent decades. It should be able to continue to do so.

China's Growing Demand for Energy and Other Natural Resources

On a per capita basis, China is poorly endowed with most natural resources. Per capita availability of arable land, for example, is only 0.095 hectares, 60 percent below the world average; per capita availability of water is 75 percent below the world average; and per capita availability of most key mineral resources is well under half the world average.[20] The only important natural resource of which China's per capita availability is relatively high is coal.

The combination of modest natural resource endowments and rapid sustained growth has rendered China increasingly dependent on imports to satisfy its basic needs for petroleum and a broad range of other natural resources. Between 1995 and 2005, China's energy consumption rose 80 percent, even as domestic oil production growth slowed. Consequently, China now relies on imports to meet almost half its petroleum demand. According to the International Energy Agency, while China accounted for under a tenth of global petroleum demand, it accounted for slightly more than a third of incremental world oil consumption over 2002 through 2004, contributing materially to upward price pressure in global markets.[21]

The earlier examples of Japan, Korea, and Taiwan show that severe resource constraints are not necessarily an impediment to rapid, sustained economic growth. As long as the global economy remains open, the raw materials and resources necessary for rapid economic growth can be imported. Indeed, China's bill for its net imports of energy and other primary products in 2004 was only 4 percent of its GDP—less than the 5 percent level that prevailed in Japan and Taiwan at the beginning of their high growth in the mid-1960s, and less than half the levels these countries hit by the late 1970s, when energy prices had soared.[22]

China, however, faces the additional problem that its rapidly rising demand for basic energy and mineral resources stems not only from rapid growth but, more importantly, from inefficient resource use. For example, China's energy consumption per unit of output is more than double the world average. Thus, while China's GDP in 2005 was only one-seventh that of the United States, its consumption of primary energy was slightly more than half the U.S. level.

On July 6, 2005, China's cabinet, the State Council, issued a special document calling for new measures to conserve energy, water, and raw materials.[23] The new initiative's underlying premise is that without a major change in the pattern of resource use, it will be difficult for China to sustain its pace of economic growth and to promote a clean and healthy environment. The State Council's report embodies some of the recommendations the National Reform and Development Commission made in late 2004—for example, that China adopt energy savings policies and technologies that would allow it to quadruple its economic output by 2020 but only double the level of energy consumption over the same period.[24] A similar goal has been incorporated in the Suggestions for the Eleventh Five-Year Program approved by the Chinese Communist Party Central Committee in October 2005, which calls for a 20 percent reduction in the consumption of energy per unit of output by 2010 compared with 2005.[25]

While some believe this target may be hard to meet,[26] it is important to recognize that since the beginning of reform, China has reduced substantially the amount of energy required to produce each unit of GDP. Compared to 1978, by 2004 China produced three and a half times as much output for each ton of standard coal equivalent of energy consumed.[27] That implies a 4.9 percent average annual reduction in energy intensity of economic activity. Almost all of this improvement reflects changes in real energy intensity, rather than simply a change in the output mix in favor of products that require less energy to produce. Thus, while China is less energy efficient than many other countries, its trajectory over time has been favorable.

The most important challenge in maintaining that favorable trajectory is energy pricing policy. In the early 1980s, when China was still self-sufficient in oil, the domestic price of crude was about one-sixth the international price. Refined petroleum products were under-priced as well. One important factor stimulating increased efficiency in the use of energy in the 1990s was China's policy of gradually raising the domestic price of crude oil and refined petroleum products, starting in the late 1980s. By June 1998, convergence of domestic and international prices was complete: China's State Council adopted a formal policy of pricing domestic crude oil at the international price and not allowing any price subsidies for refined petroleum products sold at the retail level.

When global crude oil prices began to rise sharply in 2004, however, the government modified this policy. Domestic crude was still priced at the international level, but the government, by limiting retail price increases, increasingly insulated consumers of refined products from the rising global cost of crude oil. For example, in the first nine months of 2005, when the global price of crude rose by three-fifths, China passed through only about one-third of the increase to the prices of refined petroleum products.[28] As a result, refined product prices in China in late 2005 were the lowest of any major global economy—roughly one-third below U.S. levels, which by a wide margin are the lowest of any advanced industrial economy.

That pricing policy introduced a major distortion. China's energy companies are still paying the much higher international price for crude oil, but because they have been unable to pass along the increased costs, they suffer from severely squeezed margins. Their response by mid-2005 was to start selling large quantities of refined product back into the international market, where prices were much higher than on the domestic market. The predictable result was a domestic shortage of refined product, particularly in south China. At mid-year the government had to step in and prohibit refiners from signing new export contracts. Ultimately the government had to provide offsetting subsidies to compensate refiners for their economic losses on the domestic sale of refined petroleum products. China's largest refiner, Sinopec, for example, received a $1.2 billion subsidy at year-end 2005.

China is unlikely to be able to continue on its long-term trajectory of increased energy efficiency unless it ends its policy of largely insulating domestic consumers of refined products from higher prices. Moreover, hard budget constraints will have to be imposed on the significant minority of state-owned enterprises that are earning less than their cost of capital. These firms need to be fully subjected to the discipline of the market, and thus become more sensitive than at present to relative prices and measures of profitability.

Agricultural Challenges

China occupies only 7 percent of the world's arable land, yet must feed about a fifth of the world's population. Not surprisingly, food security has long preoccupied China's leaders, not only since 1949 but in the imperial era as well. The challenge of managing the farm sector has grown with China's WTO commitments in agriculture, which are more far reaching than those of other developing countries and in certain respects exceed those of high-income countries. The Chinese government agreed to reduce tariffs and institute other policies that meaningfully increase market access; accepted tight restrictions on the use of agricultural subsidies; and pledged to eliminate all agricultural export subsidies—commitments that go far beyond those made by other participants in the Uruguay Round negotiations that led to the WTO's creation.[29]

In short, China's leadership has largely jettisoned the traditional objective of agricultural self-reliance, which was inefficient in economic terms, in favor of much greater reliance on international markets.[30] At one level, this strategy appears to have succeeded. China has become a large net importer of land intensive crops such as soybeans and cotton, in which it has little or no comparative advantage, while becoming a large net exporter of a broad range of higher value-added and more labor-intensive commodities, such as horticulture, animal, and aquaculture products. Over the same period, however, income inequality in the farm sector has increased sharply. The share of the farm population earning more than twice the average farm income doubled between 2000 and 2004, and the pace at which rural residents are escaping poverty has slowed dramatically.[31]

Fiscal Challenges

China's fiscal position seems strong when compared with many emerging markets. The government's budget deficit in the past four years has averaged less than 2.5 percent of gross domestic product and fell to only 1.5 percent in 2004.[32] Meanwhile, the total stock of government bonds outstanding at year-end 2004 was only RMB 3.5 trillion. This is a relatively modest one-quarter of GDP compared to a government debt to GDP ratio in the United States that is over three-fifths.

Yet lurking behind this façade of fiscal rectitude is the state's massive accumulation of implicit fiscal obligations. This includes the indebtedness of provincial and sub-provincial governments, which is not counted in the tally given above; the indebtedness of state-owned asset management companies, which the government created in 1999 to deal with the massive accumulation of nonperforming loans in state-owned banks; the non-performing loans that remain on the books of state-owned banks; and unfunded state pension liabilities. Even without the last item, these contingent liabilities at year-end 2003 stood at about RMB 10 trillion, an amount equivalent to 85 percent of gross domestic product that year.[33] These contingent liabilities eventually must be financed, raising the question of how long China's fiscal position can be sustained.

A detailed analysis strongly suggests that even if all these contingent liabilities were made explicit and financed through the government budget, China would not necessarily experience an endlessly rising debt-to-GDP ratio, the prospect of which could lead to a domestic debt crisis like the one that engulfed Russia in 1998. Avoiding a fiscal meltdown, however, depends on two critical factors. First, over the long run, China must sustain the past decade's steady increase in the ratio of tax revenues to GDP. That is essential to provide the government with the budgetary resources to increase the provision of social and other services on the one hand, and pay the interest on a higher level of government debt on the other, without steadily increasing the budget deficit. Second, China's banks must rapidly strengthen their credit culture and earnings so that any future non-performing loans that emerge can be written off from the banks' own earnings. Banks cannot continue to absorb state capital at anything like the pace of recent years if China's fiscal position is to be sustained.

Social Policy

Major social challenges include health care, education, unemployment insurance, and pensions. Traditionally, many social services were provided by state-owned enterprises. For example, in the early years of reform, about two-thirds of all hospital beds were in hospitals that were run as ancillary activities of government-owned businesses. Similarly, most pensions were paid directly by factories and financed on a pay-as-you-go basis from firms' current earnings, rather than through a scheme of pooled contributions managed by the state. As a result, the government was extremely reluctant to allow state-run factories to fail, since it meant the firms' retirees would immediately lose their pensions.

Reform, particularly in the last decade and a half, has severely disrupted this system as market pressures have driven many state-run businesses into bankruptcy or forced them to abandon their social service provider role. In response, the government has sought to develop alternative delivery mechanisms for many social services. Starting in 1996, for example, a new pension system was introduced which covers all urban workers, not just those working for state companies. In addition, the government has sought to mitigate the virtual collapse of the rural health care delivery system by initiating a rural cooperative medical scheme in 2002. However, these new delivery mechanisms have developed only unevenly, leaving many unemployed Chinese beyond the reach of the emerging social safety net.

This is particularly evident in the health care sector. Between 1980 and 2004, the share of health costs covered directly through the government budget fell from 36 percent to only 17 percent; meanwhile, the share financed through enterprise run health insurance schemes fell from 43 percent to 27. The net result is that the out-of-pocket burden paid directly by patients increased from 21 percent to 56 percent of total costs. Over the whole period from 1980 to 2004, while health care expenditures rose substantially, private individual expenditures accounted for two-thirds of the increase. The consequence is that access to health care has become increasingly unequal.

Yet, even this difficult challenge can be met. China's total expenditures on health care are less than 6 percent of GDP—below the average for China's peer group—and government health expenditures account for less than 5 percent of budgetary expenditures. Modestly raising this latter ratio could stabilize the share of health care expenditures households finance from their disposable income. And, as noted earlier in this chapter, a policy of increasing budgetary expenditures on health, as well as other social programs, is consistent with the government's broader macroeconomic objective of transitioning toward a more consumption driven pattern of economic growth.

Looking ahead over the next five to ten years it would be prudent for the United States to base its own strategy on the assumption that China will continue to grow rapidly and become an ever more significant factor in the global economy. China faces many domestic economic challenges and a significant economic slowdown for several years or even a collapse cannot be entirely ruled out. But the strong likelihood is that China's leadership will undertake the further reforms necessary to meet its economic challenges. This, in turn, strongly underlines the importance of the United States putting its own economic house in order, as outlined in Chapter 1 and discussed further in Chapter 4.

3

China's Domestic Transformation: Democratization or Disorder?

Social change, demographic inevitabilities, and the downside consequences of unprecedented economic growth preoccupy Chinese leaders by day and keep them awake at night. Understanding these domestic developments and the Chinese authorities' response is the most critical part of the China puzzle. China's domestic situation profoundly influences Chinese policies abroad, and will largely determine the kind of China the world faces in ten to twenty years. Moreover, Americans and Chinese share many common interests in helping assure the country's dramatic domestic transformation results in a more open, just, stable, and prosperous China in the years ahead.

DISGRUNTLED AND DISAFFECTED: DOES SOCIAL UNREST THREATEN NATIONAL STABILITY?

There has been a striking increase in the number of "mass group incidents" in China, including strikes, demonstrations, sit-ins, traffic-blocking, and building seizures—up from about 8,700 in 1993 to 87,000 in 2005.

Statistics from the Ministry of Public Security indicate that protests are growing in average size from 10 or fewer persons in the mid-1990s to about 52 people per incident in 2004. In the first half of 2005, there were 341 large-scale, organized mass incidents—17 of which involved more than 10,000 protestors—during which a total of 1,740 people were injured and 102 people killed, resulting in an economic loss estimated at 34–40 billion *renminbi*—approximately $4.2–5 billion by current exchange rates. Between January and October 2005, 1,826 police were injured and 23 killed handling mass incidents.[1]

In urban areas, sources of unrest include unfair working conditions in enterprises; lack of social security for laid-off workers; unpaid pensions for retired workers of state-owned enterprises; low and unpaid wages for migrant workers; insufficient compensation for resettled urban residents; and ethnic tensions. In rural areas, where the frequency and scale of incidents are greater, unrest arises largely from shady land confiscation, fees, tolls and other local tax burdens, environmental degradation, and official corruption. According to a 2005 report from the Chinese Academy of Social Sciences, 40 million peasants have been forced off the land to make way for roads, airports, dams, factories, and other public and private investments, with an additional two million to be displaced every year.[2] In more prosperous coastal areas where demand for land is booming, farmers are routinely undercompensated for their land, as corrupt local officials often collude with developers. Faced with relocation, rural populations have little recourse but to take to the streets.

Recent Incidents of Unrest in China

- October 2004: A clash between Han Chinese and Hui minorities in Hunan Province involving over 10,000 people left as many as 100 people dead, including 15 police, and 400 injured.
- October 2004: Over 5,000 retirees from a state-owned textile factory in Bengdu City, Anhui Province, demonstrated for higher pensions, housing subsidies, and health care.

- November 2004: Workers at one factory in Dongguan, Guangdong Province, took their bosses hostage, and workers at another factory in the same town fought with security guards, to protest layoffs.
- November 2004: One woman's anger over the cost of bridge tolls in Jieyang City, Guangdong Province, led 30,000 people to riot, confronting hundreds of police and paramilitary units, leaving one person dead.
- April 2005: In Huaxi, Zhejiang Province, frustrated with local government indifference over soil and water pollution and subsequent health problems caused by nearby chemical plants, some 60,000 farmers erupted in protest. Two people were reported killed in the violence.
- December 2005: In Dongzhou Village, Guangdong Province, local police opened fire, killing as many as 20 people during a confrontation with some 300 villagers protesting construction of a local power plant.
- January 2006: A Chinese farmer detonated a suicide bomb in a courthouse in Gansu Province, killing himself and four others and injuring 22 people. The farmer was protesting a court ruling over a land dispute.

Source: Various Chinese and Western media reports.

Central Party and government leaders are acutely aware of the challenges posed by social unrest, especially in rural areas. In a frank admission of the need to address the "factors of instability and unhealthiness that emerged in economic operations," the new Eleventh Five-Year Program highlights the need for "all-round, coordinated and sustainable development" in order to improve social welfare.[3]

A part of this strategy foresees massive infrastructure investments and construction of hundreds of new urban centers in China's central and western hinterlands to absorb excess rural labor and improve standards of living. But this approach to development might create as many problems—environmental damage, land confiscations, graft—as it solves.

In response to public protests, authorities appear to have

adopted a somewhat more permissive and sophisticated strategy, which concedes moderate levels of discontent and protest as inevitable social outcomes at China's current state of development. On occasion, central leaders step in on the side of protestors. In April 2005, Premier Wen Jiabao reportedly called a halt to construction of a dam on the Nujiang River in Yunnan Province amidst widening public outcry against the project.[4] But in the most troubling and persistent cases, local authorities intimidate or arrest individuals deemed to be "ringleaders" as a way to suppress protests.

Chinese propaganda authorities also maintain a tight grip on media reporting of mass incidents, to help prevent protests in one area from emboldening discontent in another. However, more sophisticated protestors have learned in recent years how to make use of both Chinese and foreign media, including print, broadcast, and Internet media, as well as mobile telephones, to promote their causes, expose wrongdoing, and report on localized unrest and violence.

While incidents of unrest are frequent and widespread—and clearly worrisome to Chinese leaders—they remain largely spontaneous, unorganized, and focused on localized "backyard" grievances. They probably do not threaten the stability of the regime for the near- to medium-term. The vast majority of protests are not promoting broader political reforms, nor do they appear linked through any national network or other coordinating mechanism of dissent. Chinese authorities vigorously respond at the first sign of such associations among leaders and organizations involved in protests.

IS CORRUPTION THE END OF THE PARTY?

In parallel with economic growth and greater sociopolitical openness in China, corruption has increased dramatically. According to Transparency International's Corruption Perceptions Index for 2005, China scores 3.2 on a scale of 1 to 10, with 10 being least corrupt, and ranks 78th out of 158 countries surveyed.[5] Meanwhile, public anger over rising corruption among local officials is a major cause of increasing social unrest.

In his March 2005 report to the National People's Congress (NPC), China's chief prosecutor disclosed that 11 officials at the provincial or ministerial level were among the 2,960 officials at or above the county level investigated for corruption in 2004. The Central Discipline Inspection Commission, which investigates corruption within the Party, handled 166,705 corruption-related crimes and punished 170,850 Party members, including 16 provincial and ministerial officials. A total of 345 procurators and 461 judges were also convicted for corruption during the same period. China punished over 1,600 employees of financial institutions in the first half of 2005 for fraud and other related crimes. Of these, 570 managers and branch heads have been imprisoned or fired.

In January 2005, the Chinese Communist Party ("CCP" or "Party") launched an old-style rectification campaign, partly in order to address corruption as well as the general "moral degeneration" of its members, with particular emphasis at the local level. However, in a story that repeats itself across the full range of government activity, enforcement is a problem for both political and practical reasons.

Yet, as bad as corruption has become in China, and in spite of the concerns top Chinese leaders openly express, how much of a threat does it pose to the CCP and to social stability in China?

It seems clear that, an increase in high-profile prosecutions notwithstanding, corruption occurs because officials and powerful businesspersons can get away with it. The Chinese political and legal system lacks across-the-board accountability, checks and balances, and competency, or even a quasi-independent anti-corruption agency. Problems also result from tensions between central and local interests, the ability of the latter to skirt the rules and conceal wrongdoing, and Beijing's inability or unwillingness to target the necessary law enforcement resources.

Even more broadly, however, the main causes of corruption may be structural, arising from the "distortions during a necessary transformation of the state's role in society and the economy that is taking place."[6] More troubling still is the possibility that corruption is so deeply engrained and lucrative that occasional enforcement campaigns are not sufficient to build the necessary "ethics infrastructure," but rather purely political efforts to portray the Party as "doing something."

China's economy at present apparently pays little price for corruption. The economic losses corruption causes are astonishing—as high as an estimated $84.4 billion or 5 percent of GDP in 2004.[7] But foreign direct investment has not fallen as a result and China's economy continues to outperform most of the rest of the world.

Although the Party's inability to control corruption has undoubtedly damaged its reputation, the problem does not yet pose an imminent threat to its ruling status. The central leadership, with its open appeals to combat corruption, has been largely successful in casting itself as an opponent of corruption and defender of the "little guy" who bears the brunt of local-level malfeasance. This approach can probably be sustained as long as economic prospects are good for the majority of citizens, the CCP continues its high-profile anti-corruption campaigns, and disgruntlement arising from official wrongdoing remains localized and contained.

CAN THE BURDENS OF POPULATION AND DEMOGRAPHY BE DEALT WITH?

China's population of 1.3 billion is an implacable burden for the country's political, social, and economic development. Keeping such a sizeable population fed, clothed, sheltered, and generally satisfied consumes enormous resources in itself. But beyond the sheer enormity of China's populace, certain other population and demographic trends have a multiplier effect in exacerbating China's host of socioeconomic challenges.

China's Floating Population

Scores of millions of Chinese peasants—China's "floating population"—are abandoning the countryside in the poorer central and western provinces and flocking toward urban areas in search of economic opportunity. According to data released by China's

National Population and Family Planning Commission, the number of internal migrants increased from about 53.5 million in 1995 to over 140 million in 2004, and will continue to grow for the near term. Migrant workers today account for about 20 percent of China's working age population (15–64 years old).

Rural-to-urban migration is a double-edged sword for China. Migration enables surplus rural labor to find urban jobs and accumulate savings, and remittances from migrant workers are an important source of income for poorer family members who stay behind. Areas that employ migrant workers benefit from a ready supply of cheap labor, which has contributed to rapid economic growth in urban areas, particularly in the light industrial sector.

However, large-scale migration rapidly increases the rate of urbanization in China, bringing challenges including environmental pollution, health and sanitation problems, and social unrest, as migrant workers increasingly protest harsh working and living conditions. Homelessness, indigence, and petty crime are on the rise in Chinese cities, in part a result of the influx of itinerants from the countryside. Vast migrant worker "towns" are springing up on the edges of major cities where China's domestic challenges come together in microcosm: weakening social safety net; environmental, health, and sanitation troubles; poverty; and rising levels of disaffection. Recognizing these challenges, the State Council in January 2006 passed new guidelines on the protection of rural migrant workers' rights, including timely wage payment and provision of education to their children.

Yet China's workforce will not grow forever. According to the United Nations' projections, China's working-age population will soon begin to shrink after peaking around 2015 (see Figure 3.1). Labor shortages have already begun to surface in some parts of China, such as in Guangdong Province.[8]

Graying China

Unlike the West and other developed economies, which became "rich" before they became "old," China will be the first major country to become "old" *before* it becomes "rich."[9]

FIGURE 3.1 Change in China's Working-Age Population (Aged 15–59) by Decade

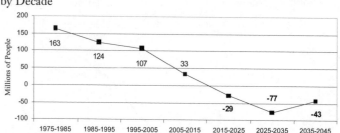

Source: United Nations Population Division, 2004 U.N. data, *World Population Prospects: The 2004 Revision Population Database,* http://esa.un.org/unpp, accessed January 24, 2006.

Two fundamental forces drive China's aging population trend—falling fertility and rising longevity. The total fertility rate (TFR) of Chinese women has decreased dramatically from 6.1 in 1949 to 1.8 in 2002—below the 2.1 birthrate required to keep the population steady.[10] Today, China's TFR pattern matches that of more developed countries, and the country claims one of the lowest fertility rates in the world. This is partly the result of the Chinese government's one-child policy, introduced in 1979. A more important factor is China's overall socioeconomic modernization, which, as shown across the world, results in significantly reduced birthrates.

China's rapid socioeconomic development has also enabled noticeable improvements in public hygiene, nutrition, health care, and life expectancy. As a result, despite the fact that only 11 percent of China's present population is over 60, the United Nations projects that the proportion of elderly will increase to about 28 percent in 2040, by which time over a quarter of the world's elderly population will live in China. The projected share of elderly in the population will begin to exceed that of the United States in 2030 (see Figure 3.2). In terms of absolute numbers, with 134 million people over 60 years old, China already has the world's largest elderly population. That figure is likely to hit about 397 million by mid-century.[11]

China has yet to develop a successful and well-funded pension system, and hence the great majority of Chinese continue to rely

FIGURE 3.2 Percentage of the Elderly (Aged 60 & Over) in China and the United States by Decade

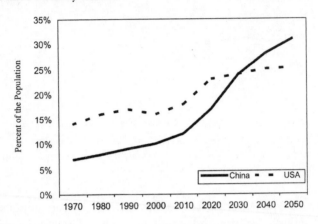

Source: United Nations, *World Population Prospects: The 2004 Revision Population Database*, http://esa.un.org/unpp, accessed January 24, 2006.

on the traditional form of old-age insurance: children. Ten years from now, as China's baby boomers begin to retire, the first single-child generation will assume the burden of caring for the elderly—not just two parents, but four grandparents as well. This informal safety net will come under increasing pressure as the population ages. Looking beyond individual families, there is also a decline in working-age adults aged 15 to 59 in China for every elder aged 60 and over. According to projections by the United Nations, the number will fall from six at present to just two in 35 years (see Figure 3.3).

Skewed Gender Ratio: From Boys to Men

China faces the starkest gender imbalance in the world. The global norm for male-female sex ratio at birth is 105 boys to 100 girls. According to China's 2000 national census, the country's ratio increased to roughly 117 males for every 100 females.[12] This skewed ratio results from the one-child policy, the tradi-

FIGURE 3.3 Ratio of Working-Age Chinese (Aged 15–59) to Elderly Chinese (Aged 60 & Over) by Decade

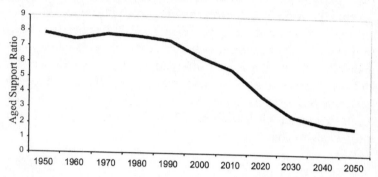

Source: United Nations, *World Population Prospects: The 2004 Revision Population Database,* http://esa.un.org/unpp, accessed January 24, 2006.

tional preference for a male child, advances in sonogram technology to determine the sex of fetuses, and widespread availability of abortion in China (sex-selective abortion is illegal in China, but occurs nonetheless). Female infanticide is also practiced, though it is difficult to calculate.

Some experts believe China's growing population of single men—perhaps as many as 30 million by 2020—may threaten the country's prospects for stability.[13] The increasing surplus of bachelors is potentially a source of social stresses; for example, it could fuel the sex trade and the trafficking in brides from other Asian countries.

PUBLIC WELFARE: WHAT HAPPENED TO THE SOCIAL SAFETY NET?

As China's socioeconomic system moves increasingly toward the market and the role of the state diminishes as a provider of social services and public goods, the country's education, health, and social safety net systems—traditionally core aspects of Chinese socialism—have suffered. Moreover, with the central government cutting back on financial support to localities, poorer and rural parts of China are particularly hard-pressed to subsidize decent education, health care, and other social benefits.

On the other hand, the government's steady retreat from provision and oversight of social welfare activities has opened up new demand and social space for alternative, private-sector services and organizations, such as businesses, entrepreneurs, and non-governmental organizations (NGOs), to fill this need. This has led to a greater pluralization of Chinese society, a trend that looks likely to continue.

Education

China's pre-university public education system is the largest in the world. According to official statistics, in 2003, over 213 million students were enrolled in over 515,000 public primary, junior secondary, and senior secondary schools throughout the country. The government also regulates and encourages private educational organizations to meet undersupplied niches in the market. With government encouragement, private education has taken off in China: in 2004, China had 78,500 private institutions, particularly in major cities, enrolling 17 million students.[14]

Since 1986, Chinese law has required nine years of mandatory education for all Chinese children. According to Ministry of Education estimates in 2004, more than 93 percent of the country has achieved nine-year basic education. Illiteracy rates have also declined steadily; the nationwide average was approximately 10.95 percent in 2003, down from 21.7 percent in 1990.[15] In 2004, the total amount of national education spending increased by 16.66 percent from the previous year, and accounted for 2.79 percent of GDP.[16]

However, these overall trends are unbalanced, and reflect disparities seen elsewhere in China where urban and coastal areas benefit far more than China's poorer, rural regions. Illiteracy tends to be more concentrated in the less-developed central and western regions. In general, rural areas are unable to retain and attract talented teachers, and poor rural localities typically charge student fees to help cover costs of books, food, uniforms, and housing.[17] Almost all of the students who do not finish their compulsory schooling live in poor rural areas, where many families struggle to obtain sufficient funds to attend school. In rural and ethnic communities, where the one-child policy is more flexible, families with more than one child often face the difficult choice of schooling one but not the others; girls often lose out in this choice.

Higher education, especially at China's top-tier universities, presents a different story. In 2004, there were 2,236 institutions of higher education across the country, with a total enrollment of 20 million students.[18] The central government has identified key universities to build into first-rate and world-class institutions through special initiatives that aim to create 100 top Chinese universities for the twenty-first century. Other initiatives will focus on a few key universities, such as Beijing University, Tsinghua University, and Fudan University, through very concentrated high-level funding.

Health and the Social Safety Net

Health conditions in China have improved considerably over the past 50 years. According to statistics from the World Health Organization (WHO), the average life expectancy of people in China has been raised from 35 in the 1950s to 71 in 2003. The mortality rate of Chinese infants declined from as high as 20 percent during periods in the twentieth century to 2.5 percent at present. For the most part, China's improved health situation is attributable to its rapid economic development and public-financed disease prevention strategy.

Despite these gains, China's public health sector faces a number of challenges. As China moves steadily toward a market-oriented health care system, the government has failed to establish a substitute for the old "collective" health care system. Today, private spending on health care represents almost twice as much as public health care spending as a percentage of GDP.[19]

As a result, according to a 2005 report released by China's State Council Development Research Center, the country's medical insurance system currently covers less than half of urban residents (approximately 100 million people) and only 10 percent of the rural population. The same report also notes that "China's medical reform has been unsuccessful because it has become unbearably expensive to patients and many dare not go to the hospital when they fall ill."[20]

In addition, the disparity in government health care spending between urban and rural areas is stark and increasing. United Nations' data show the average level of per-capita health spending in urban areas was more than twice the national average and 3.5 times the average health spending level in rural areas. China's medical resources have been mostly allocated to benefit urban areas, while the lack of funding in rural areas means poor and declining health services over time.

With an ailing public health care system, China is increasingly vulnerable to the spread of infectious diseases. There are some 200 new HIV infections a day in China, with a total official estimate of 650,000 HIV-positive persons in China at the end of 2005. The increase in China's sex trade, increasing pre-marital and extra-marital sex, and risky behavior in the "floating population" of migrant workers could serve as a bridge to spread the epidemic into the general population.[21] In some provinces, such as Yunnan, Henan, and Xinjiang, HIV prevalence rates exceed 1 percent among pregnant women, and among persons who receive premarital and clinical HIV testing, meeting the United Nations criteria for a "generalized epidemic."[22]

Avian influenza, or "bird flu," is another concern. Since China first acknowledged one case of bird flu in July 2004, the virus has spread among chickens in numerous villages in southern and western China. In 2005, Chinese agriculture authorities reported 32 outbreaks in poultry in 12 provinces, resulting in the culling of more than 24 million birds.[23] The government announced China's first confirmed human cases at the end of 2005. As of February 2006, the Chinese Ministry of Health had announced 14 confirmed human cases, eight of which have been fatal.

Chronic and non-communicable diseases are also a serious problem. A 2005 WHO projection estimates that over the next decade, over 80 million people will die from chronic diseases in China, a remarkable increase of 19 percent over the previous decade. It is projected that China will lose $558 billion over the next decade from premature deaths due to heart disease, stroke, and diabetes.[24]

Other lagging health-related factors contribute to this toll. According to the United Nations Development Program, for example, only 44 percent of China's population had "sustainable access to improved sanitation" in 2002, and some 23 percent of the population in 2002 did not have "sustainable access to improved water sources."[25]

China's current health care and retirement system do not provide a social safety net to replace the "iron rice bowls" that once guaranteed China's state-employed population with "cradle to grave" benefits, including a modicum of preventative measures and health care treatment. According to data from the Chinese Ministry of Labor and Social Security and other estimates, in 2002, only 55 percent of the urban workforce and 11 percent of the rural workforce were covered by China's public pension systems.[26] The challenges of an aging population, as well as the increase in chronic and infectious diseases, threaten to overwhelm an already inadequate social welfare system.

WHAT IS CHINA'S ENVIRONMENTAL FORECAST?

While distinctive in scale and in the amount of international attention it received, the Songhua River benzene spill in November 2005 was not an isolated incident. Rather, the Songhua case exemplifies the drivers behind nearly all environmental problems in China—local government protectionism, insufficient government transparency, weak and understaffed environmental enforcement agencies, and a pervasive lack of mechanisms for informing and involving the public in environmental protection issues.

China's economic explosion has created an ecological implosion. Severe air and water pollution along with water shortages are threatening human health, industrial production, and crops.

Land degradation and deforestation are exacerbating floods and desertification, as well as endangering the country's rich biodiversity. Pan Yue, the vice-minister of the State Environmental Protection Agency (SEPA), stated frankly that China's economic miracle is a myth, since environmental degradation is costing the country nearly 8 percent of its annual GDP.[27]

Sixteen of the world's twenty most air-polluted cities are in China. Two-thirds of China's cities do not meet the country's own air emission standards. Nearly 200 cities fall short of the WHO standards for airborne particulates.[28] China's current and continuing heavy dependence on its domestic, lower-quality coal, which accounts for about 70 percent of China's energy supply, has led to serious health problems and deterioration of China's air quality. One SEPA study revealed that in the 340 cities where air quality is monitored, 75 percent of the urban residents breathe unclean air.[29] Air pollution in China is responsible for between 300,000 and 500,000 premature deaths annually. And yet the government is planning 562 new coal-fired power stations by 2012—nearly half the world's total. Another concern is dust storms that are caused by growing desertification in northern China. China's dust, which can carry other pollutants, has already begun to reach the western coast of the United States.

An even bigger source of air pollution is linked to the country's growing wealth: Auto emissions accounted for 79 percent of total air pollution in China in 2005. Car and other vehicle ownership in China trails the United States by a wide margin—with only 22 cars per 1,000 people in China as compared to 764 per 1,000 in the United States. However, since cars are becoming more affordable, the number of vehicles is rapidly increasing and will most likely rise from 24 million today to 100 million by 2020. To encourage more fuel-efficient cars, there is discussion within the government to charge high gas prices and increase taxes on larger cars. However, gas prices still remain well below the market price due to fears of social instability.

Water is another source of ecological anxiety. More than 75 percent of the surface water flowing through China's urban areas is considered unsuitable for drinking or fishing; 90 percent of urban groundwater is contaminated; and nearly 50 percent of river water is unsuitable for agriculture or industry. Meanwhile, China's agricultural production has been severely hindered by scarcity and inefficiency, particularly in northern China where grain production fell by 50 million tons between 1998 and 2004. Development pressures are also hurting land, forest, and animal species. While China already has 86,000 dams, the country still has considerable hydropower to tap, which could make a major contribution to this energy-starved country. However, a number of major dam projects planned in southwest China will destroy wild rivers and threaten China's most biodiverse ecosystems, as well as displace hundreds of thousands of ethnic minority residents. China also faces problems regarding solid and hazardous waste disposal, and growing degradation of its coastal marine areas.

As the Chinese environmentalist Ma Jun has noted, time is not on China's side.[30] There is a narrow window for China's leaders to aggressively control the serious environmental threats facing the country. Recognizing this, the Chinese government has passed numerous laws and regulations on resource protection and pollution control, as well as welcomed environmental assistance from bilateral and multilateral aid agencies and international NGOs. With international assistance, China's environmental legislation has moved from a focus on command-and-control regulation to more progressive market incentive laws.

In light of the growing energy shortage in China (in the summers of 2004 and 2005 nearly two-thirds of the country experienced brown outs) and growing air pollution problems, the government has prioritized increased energy efficiency, use of renewable energy, and diversified energy sources. The Eleventh Five-Year Program calls for improvement of the country's energy efficiency by 20 percent by 2010. This is an extremely ambitious goal and will demand considerably greater investments and incentives for new energy development, as well as better enforcement of existing and future energy efficiency codes.

The largest obstacle to strong enforcement of environmental regulations has been the devolution of environmental stewardship to local officials who prioritize economic growth over pollution control or sound resource management. SEPA's low political standing and limited staff—just over 300 employees—limits vigorous enforcement of most laws and regulations. Another shortcoming is the notable lack of citizen and NGO involvement in monitoring compliance with environmental laws.

Over the past twenty years, many international organizations have worked with the State Council, NPC, SEPA, Ministry of Water Resources, and other ministries to develop new environmental policies, regulations, and pilot projects. Besides the multilateral organizations (China is the biggest recipient of World Bank loans and grants for environmental work), bilateral aid and international NGOs have been very active in their "green" assistance to China. International assistance has been a major catalyst for enabling the expansion in number and capacity of Chinese environmental NGOs. However, in other cases, China's environmental activists and NGOs have felt pressure from local officials who tend to crack down on activism perceived as threatening economic development.

THE PARTY ADJUSTS: HOW MUCH REFORM TO STAY IN POWER?

In the face of its domestic socioeconomic challenges, the Party concedes the need for more serious political reform to accompany economic reform. But for the CCP, such measures are purely instrumental and aimed at keeping the Party in control. The key question is whether the Party, having launched down a more "reformist" path in the midst of unprecedented social change, can keep its footing on this slippery slope.

The CCP has learned the "negative" lessons of the Soviet Union's collapse as well as "positive" lessons from East Asian countries such as Singapore. These lessons reject post-Communist "shock therapies" of radical political reform, and borrow selectively from other quasi-democratic systems for a so-called "participatory democracy" that combines authoritarian Party leadership, a modest expansion of popular participation in the political process, and governance through the rule of law, while eschewing universal suffrage, true parliamentary bodies, checks and balances, and contested multi-party elections.

Such reforms serve as a kind of "release valve," and have been underway since the late 1970s. The Party has had some success in co-opting China's emerging "middle class" of entrepreneurs and intellectuals, casting some doubt on the notion that the rise of a middle class inevitably leads to the development of liberal democracy. Going forward, the CCP leaders recognize that more needs to be done to open the political system enough to retain legitimacy and support, but not so much that they lose power.

Top Nine Leaders of China

CCP Politburo Standing Committee

1. **HU JINTAO** (63) PRC President, General Secretary of the CCP, and Chairman of the Central Military Commission. Born in Anhui, engineer.
2. **WU BANGGUO** (64) Chairman, National People's Congress. Born in Anhui, engineer.
3. **WEN JIABAO** (63) Premier. Born in Tianjin, geologist.
4. **JIA QINGLIN** (65) Chairman, China People's Political Consultative Committee. Born in Hebei, engineer.
5. **ZENG QINGHONG** (66) PRC Vice President, President of the Central Party School. Born in Jiangxi, engineer.
6. **HUANG JU** (68) Vice Premier. Born in Zhejiang, engineer.
7. **WU GUANZHENG** (67) Secretary of the Central Discipline and Inspection Committee. Born in Jiangxi, engineer.
8. **LI CHANGCHUN** (61) Born in Liaoning, engineer.
9. **LUO GAN** (70) Born in Shandong, engineer.

Promoting "Inner-Party Democracy"

In September 2004, the CCP leadership frankly noted that China had reached a "critical stage in which new situations and new problems are mushrooming" and warned that the ruling status of the CCP "is by no means a natural result of the Party's founding, and will not remain forever if the Party does nothing to safeguard it."[31]

One response has been to promote "inner-Party democracy" and accountability through institutionalizing Party procedures. At each level of the Party, member input, including voting, is now required on major decisions including personnel appointments, and Party standing committees at all levels must deliver annual work reports. A proposal that local Party congresses be in session on a more regular basis, instead of meeting only once every five years, has been launched on an experimental basis.

Since the Sixteenth Party Congress in November 2002, there has been an effort to make Party procedures more transparent. The Chinese media now report on Politburo meetings as well as discuss the division of responsibilities among its members. Even the NPC has shown some signs of independent thinking since the early 1990s, and no longer unquestionably approves legislation put before it by the State Council. In 1992, 30 percent of delegates voted no or abstained on the vote to construct the Three Gorges Dam. In 2003, one-tenth of delegates voted against Jiang Zemin staying on as Central Military Commission chairman.

Institutionalization of Party procedures also aims to resolve one of the most persistent stumbling blocks for Communist parties: leadership succession. The transfer of power to Hu Jintao, Wen Jiabao, and the "fourth generation" of Chinese leadership in 2002–2003 was the smoothest and least controversial in over 80 years of Chinese Communist history.

Allowing Some Greater Openness at the Grassroots Level

Experiments with political reform at the grassroots level are more pervasive. Elections have taken place at the village level since the 1980s. Currently, elections occur in almost one million villages across China, affecting about 80 percent of the population in the countryside.[32] More competitive elections have been elevated to some township governments. Experiments with direct elections for "urban community residents committees" are being held in some parts of China as well, and other political reform experiments are underway across the country, including the system of "democratic consultation" in which ordinary citizens are free to express their concerns on important issues during open meetings with local officials.[33]

However, the Party will not allow too much of a good thing. An internal Party document reportedly found that up to 75 percent of rural Party organizations were in a "state of collapse" in the 1990s, and other entities, including "reactionary forces, both traditional clans and triads and also newly established Christian churches" were stepping into the political vacuum.[34] In 2002, the Party and State Council issued a joint circular requiring that candidates for Party branch chief must first show that they can be popularly elected as village committee chair, and allowing members of village committees to be admitted into the Party "in order to infuse rural basic-level Party organizations with new blood"—another example of Party co-optation of elites.[35] Hence the aim to "reform" and "open" the Party: not to disband it, but to reinvigorate its legitimacy and effectiveness.

Adjusting Party-State and Central-Local Relations

During the period of economic reform and opening since the 1980s, there has been a steady effort to separate Party work from "State" or governance activities, and to allow greater administrative and fiscal power to devolve from the central government to the localities. But emerging concerns in the 1990s, including the collapse of the Soviet Bloc, as well as local protectionism, corruption, and increasing unrest, provided the political and economic impetus for some reassertion of central Party and government controls in recent years, with mixed success.

Tax reforms adopted in 1994 helped improve Beijing's fiscal position and increased central government revenue as a percentage of GDP from 10.7 percent in 1995 to 18.5 percent in 2003.[36] A number of key bureaucracies at the local level are no longer under the authority of local governments but instead answer to their functional administrative superiors at the center. The Party has also raised the number of cadres subject to the nomenklatura system—a list of leading positions, appointment to which is fully controlled by the CCP. In addition, Beijing continues to downsize and reorganize its vast bureaucracy, while introducing a more centralized professional civil service system.

Despite these steps, the CCP and central authorities continue to experience problems implementing policies at the local level, especially in the effort to stem corruption. Not unlike the federal system in the United States, local officials are faced with balancing competing demands from Beijing with those of their local constituents, and seek to circumvent central commands or ignore "unfunded mandates."

Hu Jintao "Thought"?

In contrast to his predecessors—Mao, Deng, and Jiang—there is no "thought," "theory," or "important thinking" officially ascribed to Hu Jintao—yet. Hu's "populist" approach and concern for the underprivileged "losers" in China's modernization drive led some observers to mistakenly conclude that Hu is a liberal reformer. On the contrary, Hu's political ideology has more in common with China's "New Left" and their criticism of neo-liberalism. Hu has overseen the consolidation of "the guiding position of Marxism in the realm of ideology" and the establishment of a new academy for the study of Marxism in the Chinese Academy of Social Sciences in 2005. In tackling China's socioeconomic challenges, Hu aims to strengthen the Party's ability to govern not by enacting liberal democratic reforms but by getting back to its "roots" as indicated by his revival of the Maoist call for "plain living and hard struggle."

Tolerating Nongovernmental Organizations

Nongovernmental organizations, both domestic and international, also present a conundrum for the Chinese leadership. On the one hand, they can help address emerging social and environmental ills, assist in the provision of public goods and social services, and keep some tabs, limited as they may be, on local officials. They can help fill the space that has opened as the government has pulled back from social services and the market has increasingly taken over. On the other hand, the more independent and well-organized they are, the greater the perceived threat they pose to the Party. With the expansion of NGOs in China in recent years, with the "color revolutions" of the early 2000s in Georgia, Ukraine, and Kyrgyzstan, and with widening social unrest in the country, the CCP has expanded its monitoring of such organizations.

While environmental activists were among the first to establish legal NGOs in China, they are not the country's only social entrepreneurs. Over the past decade there has been an explosion of NGOs working on a broad range of issues the government has been unable or unwilling to address—rural poverty, women's rights, health care, legal aid, education, social justice for migrant workers, and assistance for the handicapped. Such bottom-up activism was facilitated by the passage of new laws in the late 1990s that created a legal framework for NGOs, for example regulations permitting up to fifty citizens to join together and create an NGO, and laws granting improved tax incentives for charitable giving.[37] Registration regulations remain fairly restrictive, however, requiring all domestic NGOs to obtain a government sponsor, forbidding them from opening branch offices in other parts of the country, or, in some cases, from having paying members. To skirt these restrictions, some groups simply register as businesses, or operate solely as Internet groups.

By 2005, according to official statistics, there were nearly 280,000 NGOs in China, excluding those unregistered.[38] However, some outside estimates calculate there are more than eight million registered and unregistered nongovernmental and quasi-governmental associations in China. These growing numbers of social entrepreneurs are essential to China's future not simply because of the services they provide, but also because they are forming the foundation for a more vibrant civil society. While environmental NGOs were the vanguard, other major areas of social entrepreneurship have opened up, including in health, legal aid, and rural development and poverty alleviation.

The increase in international NGO involvement in China has paralleled the growth in domestic NGOs. Such international groups have played a crucial role in providing funding and training to Chinese counterparts, which in turn provide the international NGOs with important information, access, and legitimacy. Over 200 international NGOs have set up offices in China and are most numerous (with over fifty groups) in the environmental sphere. The next five top areas of international NGO work are rural development, education, health, HIV/AIDS, and disability.[39]

However, in spite of some greater openness toward NGOs, the summer of 2005 saw a steady tightening of Chinese government regulation on such groups. In 2005, articles appeared in Chinese newspapers critical of "fake environmentalists" who are reportedly taking money from foreign organizations. In one scathing article, a Party Central Propaganda Department official charged NGOs with creating "mouthpieces for the United States for spurring subversion against the government."[40] The authorities have started to scrutinize activities of international NGOs that support work in China, as well as domestic NGOs that receive foreign funding. New regulations expected in 2006 will impose the same supervision and guidance requirements on foreign NGOs as are currently placed on domestic groups.

The Party appears to allow and even encourage operations of organizations carrying out charitable, social welfare, poverty alleviation, and other "non-political" work. However, organizations that are deemed "political" or seen as critical of the Party still face suppression. It is up to Party officials, often at local levels, to determine which groups are "political" and which are not.

THE PARTY AND STATE ADJUST: ARE HUMAN RIGHTS, CIVIL LIBERTIES, AND RELIGIOUS FREEDOM IMPROVING OR WORSENING?

China's record on human rights, civil liberties, and religious freedom is rightly open to criticism, both from within China and from the international community. Amnesty International reports that "tens of thousands of people continued to be detained or imprisoned in violation of their fundamental human rights and were at high risk of torture or ill-treatment" in 2005, and that "thousands of people were sentenced to death or executed, many after unfair trials." China also "continued to use the global 'war on terrorism' to justify its crackdown on the Uighur community in Xinjiang. Freedom of expression and religion continued to be severely restricted in Tibet and other Tibetan areas of China."[41] In December 2005, the United Nations Special Rapporteur on Torture concluded a visit to China and found that "the practice of torture, though on the decline—particularly in urban areas—remains widespread in China."[42] Nearly all outside observers found that in spite of improvements in some areas, there has been some backsliding in China for human rights, civil liberties, and religious freedom under the new Hu-Wen leadership.

However, even in the shadow of these darker corners of today's China, some important progress is evident. As discussed above, the new leadership team of Hu and Wen appears more cognizant of the need to expand the exercise of peoples' civil rights, and has shown some limited willingness to do so under the rubric of "participatory democracy." Beijing no longer simply dismisses international norms and concerns, and feels compelled to respond to them. Permitting the visit of the United Nations Special Rapporteur on Torture in 2005—albeit after some ten years of negotiation—was a step in the right direction.

China has ratified the United Nations International Covenant on Economic, Social, and Cultural Rights and signed, but not yet ratified, the United Nations International Covenant on Civil and Political Rights. In December 2005, despite rejecting the findings of the United Nations Human Rights rapporteur on torture, China "expressed willingness to work with him and the United Nations on future visits."[43]

The U.S. Department of State notes that China's modernization has "improved dramatically the lives of hundreds of millions of Chinese, increased social mobility, and expanded the scope of personal freedom. This has meant substantially greater freedom of travel, employment opportunity, educational and cultural pursuits, job and housing choices, and access to information."[44] China has also agreed to discuss human rights as part of the ongoing "senior leaders dialogue" with the United States, and carries out a formal human rights dialogue with the European Union as well as with several individual EU member states such as France and the United Kingdom.

But in spite of these and other encouraging steps, China has a very long way to go in developing the norms and enforcing the policies Americans would find tolerable regarding human rights, civil liberties, and religious freedom. Beijing maintains a relativist stance on what constitutes human rights, arguing they should be based on "national conditions." The Freedom House survey for 2005 ranks China at 6.5 on a scale of 1 to 7, with 7 designating the least free countries in the world. *Human Rights Watch 2005* concludes that China "remains a highly repressive state." Amnesty International and the U.S. Congressional-Executive Commission on China effectively echo these findings.

Recent years have also seen a clampdown on the press. It appears that the Hu-Wen leadership, which initially welcomed media reporting on previously taboo subjects such as official corruption and social unrest, is as willing as its predecessors to gag the media when coverage goes beyond the Party's sanctioned parameters. Reporters Without Borders termed China, as of January 2005, "the world's largest prison for journalists," and reported that in 2004 in China, 17 journalists were arrested, 65 media outlets were censored, and three repressive media laws were passed.

Similarly, the Party is struggling to come to terms with the Internet—a crucial tool for economic modernization, but one that offers some 111 million Chinese netizens unprecedented access to information not sanctioned by the authorities—and that number is growing larger by the day. The Ministry of Information Industry, Ministry of Public Security, and State Secrets Bureau among them employ an estimated 30,000 Internet police, who manage a sophisticated communications monitoring and filtering regime. The technology is backed by legal and regulatory policies enforced on Internet service and content providers, allowing the Party to censor and block access to foreign sites such as the BBC and Voice of America, as well as content related to terms such as "human rights," "Taiwan" or "Tibetan independence," and "Falun Gong." While the Chinese authorities defended their Internet controls in February 2006, claiming that they are just following international practice of blocking "harmful" websites that promote such things as pornography and terrorism, observers estimate that there are 49 "cyberdissidents" and 32 journalists currently in detention for posting on the Internet information critical of the Party.

In terms of religious freedom, the Chinese Constitution guarantees protection for "normal religious activity," a phrase that obviously lends itself to political interpretation. In its 2005 annual report, the U.S. Commission on International Religious Freedom found that the Chinese government "continues to engage in systematic and egregious violations of religious freedom" and that "prominent religious leaders and laypersons alike continue to be confined, tortured, imprisoned and subjected to other forms of ill treatment on account of their religion or belief." However, the report also notes that regulations issued by China in November 2004 allow for religious organizations to provide social services to the community, accept donations from overseas, and host inter-provincial religious meetings under certain circumstances.

The Party is most concerned with religious groups that may generate political loyalties to persons or authorities beyond its control. Such concern is greatest in Tibet and Xinjiang, where Beijing fears the longstanding mix of religious beliefs and separatist goals. According to the Tibet Information Network, as many as 135 Tibetans are imprisoned on political grounds, two-thirds of whom are monks or nuns. In the far western Xinjiang region, Beijing has likewise put down Islamic religious activities linked to separatism, especially since the late 1990s, which has had a chilling effect on religious expression. In its Central Asia policy, China officially calls for the eradication of the "three evils"—terrorism, separatism, and religious extremism—indicating how Beijing closely associates these tendencies.

So-called "Patriotic Christian Churches" are allowed relative freedom to operate. Estimates from the official Protestant Church in China state there are some 16 million baptized Protestant worshippers attending some 55,000 formally sanctioned churches, with 2,700 pastors and 18 seminaries and Bible schools.[45] Outside estimates suggest the number of Protestant worshippers is probably five times more when unofficial "house churches" and other proscribed congregations are counted. Recent research states there are about 12 million Catholics attending some 6,000 churches in China.[46] According to the U.S. Department of State, approximately 8 percent of the Chinese population is Buddhist, 1.5 percent is Muslim, an estimated 0.4 percent belongs to the official Catholic Church, an estimated 0.4–0.6 percent to the unofficial Vatican-affiliated Catholic Church, an estimated 1.2–1.5 percent is registered as Protestant, and up to 2.5 percent worship in Protestant house churches that are independent of government control. In addition, there are several hundred thousand Taoists and hundreds of millions of Chinese who engage in traditional folk religions (worship of local gods, heroes, and ancestors). Despite the crackdown, there are still thought to be hundreds of thousands of Falun Gong practitioners across China.[47]

PARTY AND STATE ADJUSTMENT: GREATER RULE OF LAW?

No one claims that China is today a rule of law country. The harsh criminal justice system is still plagued by the use of torture, aggressive defense lawyers are likely to end up as defendants themselves, and successful businesses can get expropriated by local governments.

Nevertheless, most would acknowledge that China has moved a long way from the primarily "rule of man" governance approach of traditional China, and is taking steps beyond the instrumental "rule *by* law" approach characteristic of legal reform in recent years, toward a legal system that increasingly seeks to restrain the arbitrary exercise of state and private power and does provide the promise, if not the guarantee, to assert rights and interests in reliance on law.

The Party has gradually ceded a good deal of authority to the market, the government, the courts, and other institutions that grapple on a daily basis with the complex decisions and policies required of a rapidly changing society and economy. This partial withdrawal by the Party provides a degree of political space for the development of "rule of law with Chinese characteristics." However, despite the growth of an increasingly robust legal system and legal consciousness, the Party retains ultimate control, especially over sensitive issues.

Over the past 15 years, to help curb corruption and promote economic development through improved administrative efficiency, China's leaders have progressively introduced a number of administrative mechanisms that impose legal restraints on state action and bolster public supervision of government in ways that can be enforced directly by aggrieved citizens. China's commitments to market-based regulatory reforms upon its entry into the WTO in 2001 further strengthened these efforts.

The landmark 1989 Administrative Litigation Law (ALL), fortified by the 1994 State Compensation Law (SCL), grants Chinese citizens the unprecedented right to sue the government over "concrete" government actions that violate their rights and interests, although not over "abstract" actions such as decision making. While the ALL and the SCL attempt to limit state action by providing redress after the fact, the 1996 Administrative Penalties Law (APL) and the 2004 Administrative Licensing Law impose procedural constraints on government action itself. The APL is the first Chinese law to provide regulated persons the right to defend their case and the right to a public hearing in the event the agency plans to impose a penalty such as ordering production stoppage, revoking a license, or imposing a large fine. This law thus introduced the concept of procedural due process.[48]

The importance of procedural fairness has arisen in a number of ways. Revised regulations on the handling of petitions to government agencies impose obligations to provide a response to petitioners and require for the first time in Chinese history that public hearings be held on "major, complex or difficult" problems raised by petitioners.[49] While the number of protests over land-takings and the swelling number of petitions indicate that these procedural safeguards are not yet taking hold, the trend is clear in terms of legal reform and leadership awareness of what needs to be done. Criminal law and procedure revision is on the legislative agenda of the National People's Congress, and the legal issues involved are being debated in academic, legal, and official circles as well as in the media.

By the end of 2005, provincial level governments and central ministries had held a total of 74 rulemaking hearings and 827 expert seminars and released roughly 500 draft rules for public comment.[50] Many local governments are beginning to publish virtually all draft rules and regulations for public input. Spurred by China's popularization of e-government since 1999, most governments above the county level now regularly post a great deal of information on their over 10,000 websites and hold periodic press conferences on their activities.

Breaking with the centuries-long tradition of government secrecy, the Party and government issued a joint "Opinion" establishing as national policy the presumption that all information should be made public unless exempted as a commercial secret, individual privacy, or state secret (obviously a huge loophole). At last count, over 30 Chinese provinces and large municipalities had issued locally enforceable "open government information" provisions.

Although the NPC is touted as the "highest organ of state power," in fact it has long been dismissed as a "rubber stamp" by both Chinese and Western observers. Nonetheless, recent practices reflect an effort to make the NPC and its local counterparts more professional, transparent, and responsive. People's Congress (PC) deputy elections, ostensibly democratic but in fact traditionally orchestrated by the Party, are becoming incrementally more competitive. Many deputies are now reaching out to their putative constituents for feedback, and some deputies are seeking to more effectively carry out their constitutional duties. The NPC and local PCs increasingly consult scholars and interest groups, publish draft legislation through the media to solicit broad input, and hold public hearings on draft legislation.[51] The public also has the right to file petitions with the NPC Standing Committee, challenging the legality of lower-level regulations. While this is a welcome institutional innovation, its work unfortunately has been shrouded in secrecy, and there have been no reports that any laws or regulations have yet been overturned.

China's massive judicial system of over 3,000 basic courts and nearly 200,000 judges cannot yet consistently protect the rights and interests of Chinese citizens through an independent authority to enforce government and private compliance with the law. While the courts hear roughly six million cases per year, Chinese government agencies including the courts themselves are flooded with nearly twice as many citizen petitions to resolve a range of grievances; 30 percent of these complaints are about the legal system itself and the handling of specific cases.[52]

Institutionally, the courts are answerable to the NPC, and are not an independent branch of government. The Standing Committee of the NPC, not the Supreme People's Court, has the authority to interpret national law. Judges are supposed to merely apply the law. Where the law is vague or politically sensitive issues are involved, government officials and the Party may intervene through court-based adjudication committees that supervise judges' work, and the courts may even decline to accept jurisdiction over cases. Judges are appointed and remunerated by PCs at their same level, which exacerbates the problem of local protectionism and political influence. Judicial independence is more slogan than reality in today's China.

Chinese courts also face challenges of competence and professionalism. Today, all judges are required to hold university degrees and pass a national unified law exam. However, only 40 percent of judges today hold a university degree, and the quality of judicial personnel outside the major cities like Beijing and Shanghai is very uneven.[53] Low salaries contribute to widespread judicial corruption.

A modern legal system also requires quality legal professionals to assist others in navigating legal complexities, to help improve the law, and to guide government agencies in complying with the law in their routine actions. Starting with less than 2,000 lawyers in 1979, China now claims roughly 120,000 certified lawyers and more than 300 law schools.[54]

Chinese legal scholars, many of whom study abroad, are a major source of new ideas about the role of law and legal reform in China. They and the Chinese lawyers they train are increasingly getting involved in policy making. Local PCs and government legal affairs offices frequently commission scholars' drafts and seek input from private law firms and lawyers associations. Over 400 lawyers serve as local PC deputies at all levels, and more than 1,200 serve on people's political consultative congresses.[55]

The Chinese government, law schools, and nongovernmental organizations sponsor legal aid clinics that assist low income citizens with cases involving employment discrimination, family disputes, urban relocations, and rural land grabs. More than 3,000 government-sponsored legal aid clinics claim to have aided some 1.6 million clients. For the first time in 2005, the Ministry of Justice allocated roughly $6.2 million for legal aid in impoverished areas, while local governments earmarked another $32 million.[56]

Establishing the rule of law in authoritarian China presents yet another paradox, like the creation of a "socialist market economy" or "socialist democracy." Despite the Party's refusal to relinquish ultimate power over the legal system with sometimes distressing results, the Party does seem to recognize the benefits to its own legitimacy and "governing capacity," as well as to the Chinese economy and society, in moving toward greater rule of law.

WHAT ARE THE IMPLICATIONS FOR CHINA-U.S. RELATIONS?

A host of transformative forces brought on by China's reform and opening of the past quarter century are bringing important changes to Chinese citizens' daily lives, and to the relationship among the Party, the government, and the Chinese people. Some of these changes should be welcomed; others viewed with concern. Political reform and social change in China, while positive in many respects, falls far, far short of Western-style democracy. Critical aspects of fully fledged democratic systems are woefully lacking, such as an independent judiciary, institutionalized checks and balances, opposition parties, and well-established constitutional guarantees of free speech, assembly, and religion. Reforms are primarily intended to improve the prospects of CCP rule, not undermine it.

Nevertheless, there are some bright spots in China's political reform process. New efforts are underway to democratize and institutionalize decision making. As the relationship among the Party, state, and society adjust to the realities of a more open and globalized China, new areas of expanded "social capital" are emerging, with the greater participation of NGOs and pockets of independent expression and even dissent tolerated—within limits. Encouraging progress is also being made in introducing a more predictable legal and penal system. The information revolution is making China a more open place: China has over 390 million mobile phone subscribers and 111 million Internet users.

However, if and as China moves toward a more open political system, it almost certainly will not follow a Western-style path, at least in the near term. Indeed, some research suggests that at present, there is not widespread support within the general Chinese population for Western-style democracy, and that other "preliminary steps" are more pressing: economic opportunity, clean government, and social stability.[57] While Chinese citizens may ultimately aspire to universal human values of freedom and democracy, most would also eschew "shock therapy" or disruptive political change to get there. At elite levels, Chinese academics debate the notion of a "democracy deficit," pointing to the political and economic difficulties which have followed from the rapid introduction of Western-style democracy in places such as Russia, Indonesia, Iraq, and Taiwan.

Instead, it is more likely that the Chinese leadership will continue to muddle through to deliver continued good economic prospects, maintain political power, and preserve basic order, but with a high incidence of unrest and growing socioeconomic ills and increasing openness within society over time. However, the familiar conundrum will persist: The very goals that the Chinese leadership must meet in order to maintain power, especially continued economic growth, are also the very forces which unleash demands for greater political and social change over time.

Looking ahead over the near to medium term, the United States should be prepared to deal with a China led by the Chinese Communist Party. This being the case, while calls for a more open, just, and democratic China are an indispensable part of U.S. China policy, they should be informed by realistic expectations.

Beijing's focus on managing its domestic problems presents opportunities as well as challenges for the United States. It is true that Beijing's approach to managing its domestic challenges often translates into tight political controls on information and harsh crackdowns on dissent and unrest. On the other hand, with Chinese leaders focused predominantly inward, they are less inclined toward foreign adventurism. Moreover, China's real and growing domestic challenges offer enormous opportunities for the U.S. government and private sector to export ideas, expertise, and technologies, as well as the seeds for positive political, economic, and social development in China.

Bringing about more positive social and political outcomes in China clearly calls for intensified interaction by the U.S. public and private sectors with counterparts in China to address the country's domestic concerns. These activities would involve cooperation in a range of areas, including on energy and the environment, human rights, the rule of law, good government, anti-corruption, public health, social welfare, and the role of nongovernmental organizations. The China of tomorrow will be largely shaped by what happens on its domestic front today. Given the stakes, Americans will need to devote more attention to understanding and assessing China's remarkable socioeconomic transformation and its consequences.

4

China in the World Economy:
Opportunity or Threat?

A key element of Deng Xiaoping's economic reform strategy was to abandon the Maoist ideal of national self-sufficiency and start reaping the gains available from participating in global trade. The result has been an expansion of China's trade that has outpaced the growth of its domestic economy and far exceeded the growth of global trade over almost three decades. Since reforms were launched, imports and exports as a share of China's economy have expanded greatly and China's share of global trade has grown tenfold. In 2004, China surpassed Japan to become the world's third largest trading economy, a remarkable achievement given that China's economy is only two-fifths of the size of Japan's.[1]

China's economic rise has several implications for the global economy. First, China has become a major engine of global economic growth. From 2000–2005, China's economic growth has averaged 9.5 percent in real terms; its imports have tripled from $225 billion in 2000 to $660 billion in 2005. China alone has accounted for about 12 percent of the growth of global trade, an impressively high share given that in 2000 it accounted for less than 4 percent of global trade. Indeed, although China's economy is a small fraction of that of the United States, in the first half of this decade, China's trade grew so fast that it contributed half again as much as the United States to the expansion of global trade.

China's rise also has important distributional implications for the global economy. Its massive exports of labor-intensive goods have led to significant declines in the relative prices of those goods. This, in turn, has put downward pressure on the relative wages of unskilled workers, even in advanced industrial economies. The other side of the coin is that China's imports are mostly skill- and capital-intensive investment goods, such as semiconductors and microprocessors, aircraft, machinery, and commodities such as petroleum and iron ore. Thus China's burgeoning import demand is raising the relative wages of skilled labor, the profit share of output, and commodity prices.

These patterns have important implications for the way economies at different levels of development adjust to China's rise. High-income countries, with a comparative advantage in skill- and capital-intensive goods production, are likely to find adjusting to China's economic rise less arduous than lower-income countries specializing in more labor-intensive goods production. The United States and other OECD countries are finding a growing market for their goods in China, either through exporting or through investing in manufacturing capacity in China and then selling the output in China. They face increased import competition in labor-intensive goods, such as footwear, apparel, and furniture, but output and employment in these industries have been declining for years and represent a small share of high-income economies. Low-income economies, such as India, Turkey, and Mexico, not only face import competition in key sectors of their own economies, but also the loss of exports to more competitive Chinese goods in third-country markets. Mexico during 2001–2003, for example, suffered a decline in its share of total U.S. imports as China's share increased. The decline was particularly marked in apparel and electronic equipment, products for which China's export growth has been particularly strong.[2]

This purely economic framework suggests that, in principle, the United States should find it easier than low-income countries to adjust to China's global economic rise, if still difficult in some (often politically sensitive) sectors. In practice, however, trade disputes are inherent in any high-volume trade relationship, and since the United States is China's largest trade partner and China ranks number three among U.S. trade partners, such disputes are inevitable. More important, China's massive $202 billion trade surplus with the United States, discussed in detail below, hugely exacerbates frictions, leading to more pervasive and politically significant pressures in the United States that go well beyond technical trade disputes.

Several additional factors unique to the U.S.-China relationship risk escalating bilateral trade frictions into more serious political problems. First, China is a transition economy that combines a mix of expanding market forces with a receding but still sometimes powerful government hand. Disputes can be especially difficult to resolve when one party sees a particular trade or investment outcome as generated primarily by market forces while the other sees the same result as a policy choice dictated by a state-led growth model. The bid by the China National Offshore Oil Corporation (CNOOC) for Unocal in the summer of 2005 is a case in point. The chief executive officer of CNOOC insisted that the proposed transaction was "purely commercial," while its congressional and other critics in the United States charged that China as a country was using aggressive tactics to lock up energy supplies around the world and that CNOOC's bid represented a clear threat to U.S. national security and should be blocked.

Second, China remains an authoritarian, communist state. No one can say with certainty that China's economic rise will not ultimately pose a security threat to the United States and its allies. Those who rank this as a more likely outcome naturally tend to see trade and other economic disputes through that lens, while those who rank this a less likely outcome naturally tend to see these disputes largely in commercial terms, rather than in terms of their long-term, indirect strategic implications.

Third, even if everyone were confident that China will never pose a security threat to the United States and its allies, narrow trade disputes could escalate to become a broader "China problem" because most Americans find repugnant the Chinese government's limitations on religious freedom, violations of basic human rights, and restrictions on freedom of speech, via censorship of the Internet and other mechanisms. This can make it difficult to adjudicate trade disputes in an objective manner and, in some cases, leads to U.S. trade sanctions primarily intended to influence Chinese government policy in domains other than trade, such as human rights.

While this chapter focuses primarily on China, it is important to keep in mind that the evolution of U.S.-China economic relations will be determined to an important extent by the economic performance, and indeed broader national self-confidence, of the United States. A good deal of the somewhat similar concerns in U.S.-Japan economic relations during 1970–1995 reflected the poor economic performance of the United States during that period, particularly its mediocre productivity growth of only $1-1\frac{1}{2}$ percent annually for over two decades.

Fortunately, the U.S. economy has again become the envy of the world. It has steadily expanded for 15 years, punctuated only by one brief recession in 2001. Productivity growth abruptly doubled beginning in the middle 1990s and has been sustained since. In the late 1990s, unemployment dipped below 4 percent—its lowest level in almost three decades—and remains near the "full employment" level of less than 5 percent. Inflation is mild and interest rates have remained far below their historical norms. The United States has thus regained much of its economic self-confidence and hence its proclivity, as well as its ability, to work cooperatively with the rest of the world, rather than lash out at possible threats from abroad.

The U.S. economy is far from invulnerable, however, and continuation of the rosy picture of the last decade is by no means assured. After the sizeable surplus achieved during the Clinton Administration, large budget deficits have reappeared and their future course appears ominous as the U.S. population begins to age rapidly. Domestic saving is the lowest of any large industrial country; the United States depends heavily on capital inflows from the rest of the world, including China. The current account deficit reached almost $800 billion in 2005 and is still increasing rapidly; it could at almost any point presage a large, perhaps precipitous, decline in the value of the dollar, generating additional pressure on U.S. inflation and interest rates. Continued high energy prices, or especially another upward spike, would intensify those risks. At the more structural level, U.S. primary and secondary education continues to produce results that are among the worst among all industrial—and even some developing—countries, and the rapid escalation of health care costs represents a substantial drag on the economy.

A second major problem is that, even during the recent era of good economic performance, income distribution has worsened steadily. A disproportionate share of higher incomes has accrued to those who were already well off, while the real wages of hourly American workers are lower today than in 1973. More than 40 million Americans have no health insurance. Traditional government safety nets, such as unemployment insurance, have become even less responsive to the needs of dislocated workers.

Hence, there has been a significant U.S. backlash against globalization, for which the rise of China is now the most prominent proxy. The U.S. economy is about $1 trillion per year richer as a result of the expansion of international trade over the past 60 years, and could gain another $500 billion annually if the world were to move to totally free trade.[3] But significant adjustment costs, notably job losses and lower wages for some, totaling about $50 billion per year, are also involved in trade liberalization. Thus every congressional vote on major trade legislation over the past decade has been split almost evenly, reflecting a fundamental public ambivalence over the merits of further integration with the world economy.[4]

These anxieties clearly reflect the lack of both effective transitional assistance and educational and training programs through which displaced workers can become confident of their ability to take advantage of globalization, rather than be victimized by it. Because of the new phenomenon of outsourcing of higher skill jobs, displaced workers now include white-collar as well as blue-collar workers, heightening the anxieties concerning globalization. The United States' ability to adopt and maintain constructive policies toward China (and the rest of the world) will be determined to an important extent by its success in launching new domestic initiatives to address these concerns.

WHY DOES CHINA HAVE SUCH A LARGE TRADE SURPLUS WITH THE UNITED STATES?

At or near the top of any issue list is the ever-growing deficit that the United States has in its bilateral trade with China. This issue appropriately has received more attention in recent years as China's global trade and current account surpluses have increased. In 2005, after rising modestly for several years, China's global trade surplus tripled to more than $100 billion. Meanwhile, its current account surplus soared to $161 billion—almost 7 percent of GDP, making China in dollar terms the world's second largest surplus country, only slightly behind Japan.[5]

China has had a large bilateral surplus with the United States for many years, however. Indeed, as reflected in Figure 4.1, the origins of China's bilateral surplus date back to the late 1980s. These annual deficits increased steadily in the 1990s, and by 2003 China moved into the unenviable position of being the single largest source of the overall U.S. balance of trade deficit. By 2005, the U.S. bilateral deficit with China reached $202 billion, accounting for a record 26 percent of the total U.S. global trade deficit of $782 billion. Since the ratio of U.S. imports from China to its exports to China reached an all-time high of 5.8 in 2005, U.S. exports to China would have to grow almost six times more rapidly than U.S. imports from China just to keep the trade imbalance from increasing further. As a result, many, including some in Congress, see China as having replaced Japan as the principal mercantilist trader in Asia and the major source of lost U.S. jobs, particularly in manufacturing.

The U.S. bilateral trade deficit with China is a complex and multifaceted challenge. The analysis below takes up five potential explanations of the deficit: restrictive U.S. export licensing; suggestions that China restricts access to its domestic market and pursues

FIGURE 4.1 U.S. Merchandise Trade Deficit with China, 1985–2005 (billions of $ and as a percent of the global U.S. merchandise trade deficit)

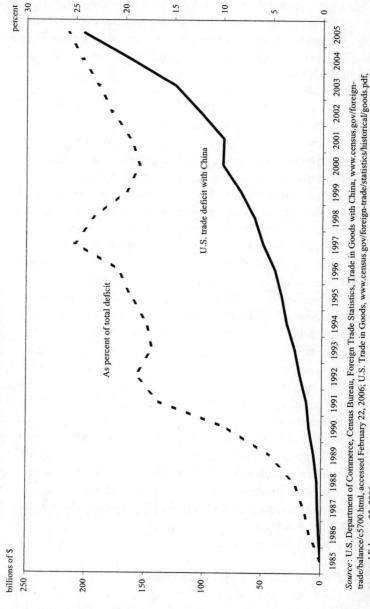

Source: U.S. Department of Commerce, Census Bureau, Foreign Trade Statistics, Trade in Goods with China, www.census.gov/foreign-trade/balance/c5700.html, accessed February 22, 2006; U.S. Trade in Goods, www.census.gov/foreign-trade/statistics/historical/goods.pdf, accessed February 22, 2006.

a mercantilist trade strategy; China's low-wage advantage; China's role in Asian production networks; and the undervaluation of the Chinese currency. These five alternative explanations are not mutually exclusive; indeed, several of them may be in play at the same time.

Restrictive U.S. Export Licensing

Chinese government officials regularly assert that the bilateral trade imbalance would be substantially less if the United States would approve more high technology exports to China. Yet, because of the liberalization of export controls over the years, very few products now require licenses for export to China, so the value of potential exports for which licenses are sought is quite small—and the Department of Commerce approves the vast majority of applications. In the 2005 fiscal year, for example, U.S. exporters applied for licenses to export products to China valued at $3 billion. The Department approved licenses covering $2.4 billion, or 80 percent of the total. It returned applications covering $590 million, for example, if they were incomplete, and denied licenses covering $12.5 million in potential sales.[6]

That means that if the Department of Commerce had approved all of the licenses rejected in FY2005, U.S. exports to China would have increased by only $12.5 million and the bilateral trade deficit would have been a mere 0.006 percent smaller. If it had approved both the rejected and returned applications, the bilateral deficit would have been reduced by only 0.3 percent.[7] In sum, the frequent claim by Chinese officials that liberalizing export licensing would significantly reduce the bilateral trade deficit does not seem plausible.

How Open Is the Chinese Economy?

The most common reason given by China's critics for the large and growing U.S.-China trade imbalance is that China is pursuing a mercantilist trade strategy, systematically restricting access to its market while aggressively supporting exports by national firms. Certainly the flood of Chinese goods into the United States, particularly into the stores of mass merchandisers such as Wal-Mart, Target, Circuit City, and Best Buy, suggests to many observers that China's high rate of economic growth is explained in large part by its recent export boom. But the appearance of huge volumes of Chinese goods in U.S. retail outlets is not sufficient to demonstrate that the Chinese economy is relatively closed to imports.

Several analytical approaches are required to examine this issue. First, of course, any evaluation of China's openness based on its trade position must be on the basis of its global trade balance or its global current account position, rather than its bilateral trade balance with the United States. There is no economic basis for preferring balanced bilateral trade; indeed the presumption is, if anything, almost certainly the opposite.

For most of the reform period, China's global current account surplus has been relatively modest. For example, as shown in Figure 4.2, in the ten-year period 1993–2002 China's current account fluctuated between a deficit of 2 percent and a surplus of 4 percent of GDP, but the average position was a surplus of only 1.6 percent. This was about half of Japan's average surplus of 2.9 percent of GDP during the decade 1984–1993, when its global surpluses loomed largest relative to the size of its economy. As already noted, however, China's current account position has risen sharply since 2002 and it now has become a major contributor to global economic imbalances.

Second, the Chinese government has materially reduced barriers to imports. For example, the average level of applied import tariffs dropped from more than 50 percent in 1982 to just under 10 percent in 2005. Compared to many developing countries, China's average import tariff rate is relatively low. As shown in Figure 4.3, China's applied import tariff rate in 2004 was 10.4 percent, compared to rates in India, Mexico, Brazil, and Indonesia of 29.1, 18.0, 12.4, and 6.9 percent, respectively. Moreover, import tariff exemptions in China are so widespread that the effective tariff ratio, that is, import tariff revenue collected relative

82

FIGURE 4.2 China's Global Trade and Current Account Positions, 1992–2005E (billions of $ and as a percent of GDP)

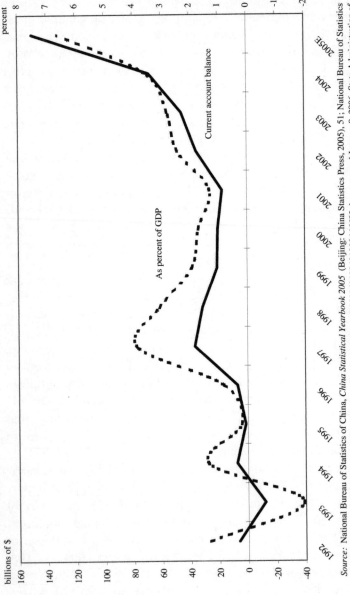

Source: National Bureau of Statistics of China, *China Statistical Yearbook 2005* (Beijing: China Statistics Press, 2005), 51; National Bureau of Statistics of China, Table of GDP at Current Prices, www.stats.gov.cn/tjdt/zygg/P020060109431083446682.doc, accessed January 9, 2006; State Administration of Foreign Exchange of China, Balance of Payments of China, www.safe.gov.cn/0430/tjsj.jsp?c_t=6, accessed September 9, 2005.

FIGURE 4.3 Applied Tariff Rates, China and Other Emerging Markets, 2004

Percent

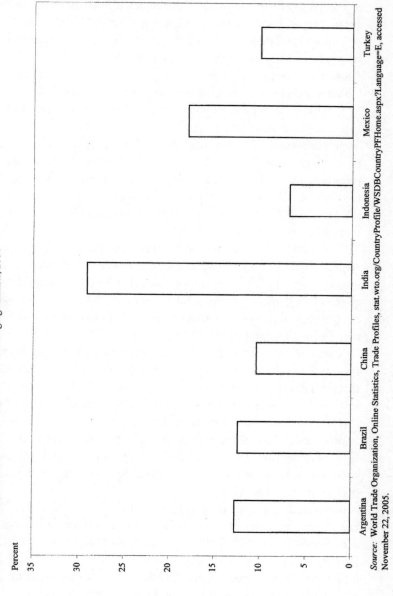

Source: World Trade Organization, Online Statistics, Trade Profiles, stat.wto.org/CountryProfile/WSDBCountryPFHome.aspx?Language=E, accessed November 22, 2005.

to the value of the imports, is very much lower than the average applied tariff. For example, as shown in Figure 4.4, the total value of import tariffs collected as a share of the value of imports fell from about 15 percent in the mid-1980s to only 2.2 percent in 2004. The effective tariff protection provided to domestic firms in China is among the lowest of any developing country.[8]

Similarly, the number of goods that the Chinese government has subject to an import licensing requirement or a specific numerical limit, such as an import quota, has dropped precipitously. At the peak in the late 1980s, the government imposed a licensing requirement on almost half of all goods imported into China. By the eve of China's entry into the World Trade Organization (WTO) in 2000, the authorities had reduced this share to less than 4 percent and, under the terms of China's accession to the WTO in 2001, the government eliminated all remaining licensing requirements in 2005. Similarly, the government eliminated all import quotas by 2005, except for those that are part of a tariff rate quota (TRQ) arrangement. China agreed to TRQs for a handful of agricultural products as part of the market opening measures it made when it joined the WTO.[9]

Third, the extent to which an economy is open can be measured by examining the ratio of imports to GDP. As shown in Figure 4.5, this ratio has soared in China, from 5 percent in 1978 to 30 percent in 2005. This ratio is roughly twice the ratio of imports to GDP in the United States and more than three times the ratio in Japan. It is also higher than other geographically large developing countries such as Argentina, Brazil, and India. Indeed only geographically small economies, such as Taiwan and Korea, have import ratios as high or higher than China.

Finally, the fact is that throughout the 1990s, China was the fastest growing export market for U.S. firms—a trend that actually accelerated from 2000–2005, as exports of U.S. firms to China rose by 160 percent while exports to the rest of the world rose only 10 percent. Indeed, China alone accounted for a quarter of the global export expansion of U.S. firms during that period.

In summary, it is difficult to sustain the charge that China's trade regime (as opposed to its exchange rate policy, about which

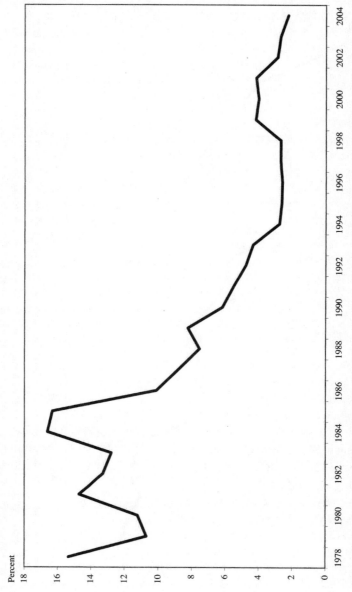

FIGURE 4.4 China's Import Tariff Revenue as a Percent of the Value of Imports, 1978–2004

Source: National Bureau of Statistics of China, *China Statistical Yearbook 1981* (Beijing: Hong Kong Economic Information & Agency, 1982), 353; *China Statistical Yearbook 1985* (Beijing: Statistical Publishing House, 1985), 494; *China Statistical Yearbook 2000* (Beijing: China Statistics Press, 2000), 258, 588; *China Statistical Yearbook 2005* (Beijing: China Statistics Press, 2005), 272, 626.

FIGURE 4.5 Imports as a Percent of GDP in China, 1978–2005

Percent

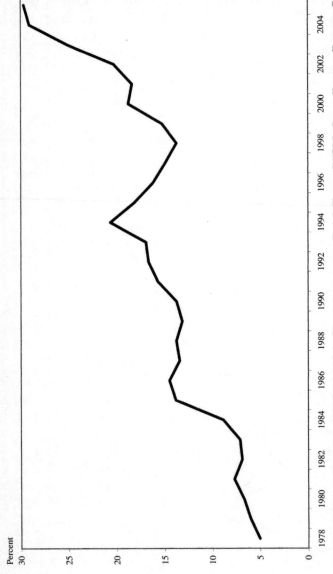

Source: World Trade Organization, WTO Online Statistics, Time Series, stat.wto.org/StatisticalProgram/WSDBStatProgramHome.aspx?Language=E, accessed November 28, 2005; National Bureau of Statistics of China, *China Statistical Yearbook 2005* (Beijing: China Statistics Press, 2005), 51; National Bureau of Statistics of China, Table of GDP at Current Prices, www.stats.gov.cn/tjdt/zygg/P020060109431083446682.doc, accessed January 9, 2006; *IMF International Financial Statistics Yearbook 2002* (Washington: International Monetary Fund), 354–355; State Administration of Foreign Exchange of China, Table of Exchange Rates of RMB, www.safe.gov.cn/0430/tjsj.jsp?c_t=3, accessed February 27, 2006.

see below) reflects the traditional mercantilist approach of restricting imports. Except for very recent years, its global current account surplus has been modest, its import tariffs are among the lowest of any developing country, and the magnitude of its imports relative to the size of its economy is growing rapidly and is relatively high.

That is not to say that expanding trade has not been a very important source of economic growth; it has been, but not because net exports, in an accounting sense, have been a major driver. Net exports have contributed positively to growth in only about half of the years between 1978 and 2005. Net exports fell, meaning trade reduced economic growth, in almost as many years as they rose. Rather, trade's contribution to China's economic growth has been indirect, through its influence on China's domestic market structure. As analyzed in Chapter 2, increased openness to trade has greatly increased competition in the domestic market, which in turn has stimulated domestic firms to become more productive.

China's Low-Wage Advantage

Some observers argue that a huge U.S. bilateral trade deficit with China is inevitable since it is simply impossible for U.S. firms to compete with firms with access to low-wage Chinese labor. There is no doubt that wages in China are very low compared to wages in the United States: The average monthly wage in manufacturing establishments in urban areas is only about $120;[10] wages in manufacturing outside of urban areas and for unskilled labor are even lower. Taking into account bonuses, incentive pay, and fringe benefits, total average hourly labor cost in manufacturing in urban areas in China is about $1, compared to almost $30 in the United States.[11]

Simply focusing on the level of wages or even on total labor cost, however, is misleading. Wages in China are low primarily because productivity is low. The World Bank, for example, calculates that average value added per U.S. manufacturing worker in

1995–99 was 28 times the Chinese level.[12] The average unskilled Chinese worker may earn only about one-thirtieth the wage of his or her U.S. counterpart, but since the productivity of a Chinese worker on average is only a small fraction of that of an American worker, the Chinese firm will not be able to sell the good in question for one-thirtieth the U.S. firm's price.

Moreover, wages are only one component of the overall cost of producing any good. Low wages are more likely to be a source of comparative advantage in industries where labor is a larger share of total costs, for example shoes and apparel, than in industries like semiconductor fabrication, in which wages are only 5 percent of total production costs. Lower labor costs are very unlikely to be a major factor favoring semiconductor production in China; indeed, as discussed below, China remains far and away the world's largest importer of semiconductors and microprocessors. On the other hand, wages constitute about 20 percent of the cost of producing apparel in the United States.[13] Firms operating in China clearly do have a comparative advantage in these products, as reflected by their very high market share in countries that do not impose quotas or otherwise restrict apparel imports.

A comparison of wages in China with those in other developing countries also confirms that wages alone do not determine a nation's competitiveness. Countries in South Asia and in sub-Saharan Africa all have wages and total labor costs that are even lower than those prevailing in China, but few firms in these countries are large exporters to the United States. For many of these countries, the productivity gap vis-à-vis U.S. workers is even greater than for Chinese workers, reflecting low levels of educational attainment and other factors. In addition, many of these countries, unlike China, have failed to provide an attractive environment for foreign investors or to invest in the physical infrastructure necessary to support large volumes of international trade. India, for example, continues to impose many restrictions on inward foreign direct investment and is currently investing only one-seventh as much as China in infrastructure.

In short, low wages of Chinese workers provide an advantage for Chinese firms in international trade, but not one that is insurmountable in many sectors where the United States maintains a competitive advantage. U.S. wages are among the highest in the world, but the United States remains the world's second largest exporter after Germany, another high-wage country. U.S. policy should be directed toward further enhancing the productivity advantage of U.S. workers, in order to maintain high wage rates in the United States, rather than trying to compete with Chinese exports of labor-intensive products.

China's Critical Role in Asian Production Networks

The single most persuasive explanation of the growing U.S. bilateral deficit is that it reflects the consolidation in China of the final assembly stage of Asian production networks. Over the past two decades, the production process for a growing range of manufactured goods has become increasingly disaggregated on a geographic basis. Each country serves as the location for the portion of the production process in which it has the strongest comparative advantage. Higher-income, more technologically advanced countries have come to specialize in producing high value-added parts and components while China, given its large pool of labor available for work in unskilled, labor-intensive operations, increasingly has become the location of choice for the final assembly of a broad range of goods, especially electronic and information technology products.

Joint ventures and wholly foreign-owned firms carry out a large portion of this assembly. Cumulative direct foreign investment in China at the end of 2005 was $610 billion, with almost two-thirds concentrated in the manufacturing sector. Most of this investment originates in other Asian economies and is in processing and assembly operations.

Goods that are assembled from imported parts and components now account for about 55 percent of China's total exports and about 65 percent of the goods China exports to the United States. When these goods are exported from China to the United States, their entire value is counted by U.S. Customs as imports from

China. In fact, on average about two-thirds of the value of these so-called "processed exports" originates outside China, mostly in other Asian countries. The assembly of notebook computers in China by Taiwanese firms, analyzed later in this chapter, provides perhaps the best example of China's growing role in Asian production networks. The key point is that the geographic disaggregation of the production process for an ever-growing volume of traded goods means that the significance of bilateral trade data is much diminished today compared to an earlier era, when most production was organized vertically rather than horizontally.

China's rise as the point of final assembly of a broad range of goods is reflected in the sharp decline over the past two decades in the share of the U.S. bilateral trade imbalance that originates in Hong Kong, Taiwan, Korea, and Japan. As these countries have moved manufacturing capacity to China—and, in the case of Japanese autos, to the United States—the share of the U.S. trade deficit that they account for has fallen by three-quarters, from more than 50 percent in 1985 to only 14 percent in 2005, while China's share has risen from nothing to one-quarter (Figure 4.6). Between 1985 and 2005, the U.S. global trade deficit as a share of GDP more than doubled, largely as a result of a further deterioration of the U.S. savings-investment balance. But the share of this deficit accounted for by the combination of China, Hong Kong, Taiwan, Korea, and Japan declined.

Undervaluation of the Chinese Currency

The fifth potential explanation of the growing U.S. bilateral trade imbalance with China is the undervaluation of the Chinese currency, the renminbi. It is important to note that China has had a growing trade surplus with the United States since the mid-1980s. But at least until 1994, by almost every available metric the renminbi was substantially overvalued rather than undervalued. Nonetheless, there can be little doubt that the increasing undervaluation of the Chinese currency since 2002 has exacerbated the underlying structural imbalance in bilateral trade—that

FIGURE 4.6 Share of U.S. Trade Deficit, by Region, 1985 and 2005 (percent)

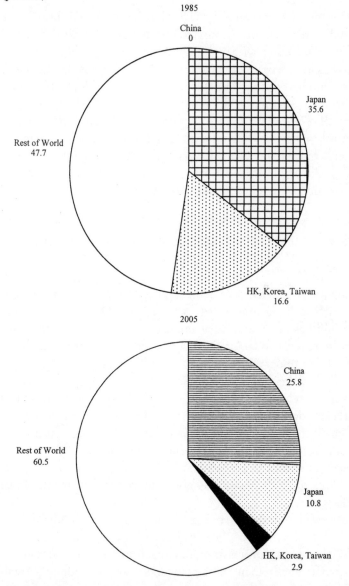

1985

China
0

Japan
35.6

Rest of World
47.7

HK, Korea, Taiwan
16.6

2005

China
25.8

Rest of World
60.5

Japan
10.8

HK, Korea, Taiwan
2.9

Source: U.S. Department of Commerce, Bureau of Economic Analysis, International Economic Accounts, U.S. International Transactions Accounts Data, Table 2. U.S. Trade in Goods, www.bea.gov/bea/international/bp_web/simple.cfm?anon=71&table_id=2&area_id=3, accessed June 30, 2006.

is, China's emergence as the main point of final assembly in Asian production networks.

This means that even if the U.S. global trade deficit shrinks, the United States is almost certain to continue to have a large bilateral deficit in its trade with China.[14] After all, the bilateral deficit grew steadily as Asian manufacturers relocated to China starting in the second half of the 1980s, even as the U.S. global trade deficit fell from its peak of $160 billion or 3.4 percent of GDP in 1987 to a low of $77 billion or 1.3 percent of GDP in 1991. Consequently, a policy focusing on achieving a sustained reduction in the bilateral trade deficit with China will almost certainly fail. The U.S. government should focus instead on policies that reduce China's global current account surplus.

WHY IS CHINA'S CURRENCY REGIME A PROBLEM FOR THE GLOBAL ECONOMY?

As noted above, in the decade through 2002, China's global current account surplus averaged 1.6 percent of GDP, suggesting the renminbi has been somewhat undervalued for some time. Since then, however, two factors have increased the extent to which the currency is undervalued. First, given China's fixed peg to the U.S. dollar, the renminbi depreciated on a real trade weighted basis after February 2002 when the value of the dollar began to depreciate significantly vis-à-vis major floating currencies such as the euro, the Canadian and Australian dollars, and the British pound. Second, even though China's productivity growth has slowed somewhat in recent years, it still exceeds its trade partners' average, thus making its goods more competitive in global markets.

As a result, China's current account surplus rose moderately to 3 percent of GDP in 2003 and to 3.6 percent in 2004. The underlying global surplus in those years, however, was undoubtedly somewhat higher than the actual one. Since economic growth was extremely rapid, demand for imported raw materials and capital goods was running at an above average rate, which meant

China's global trade and current account surpluses were smaller than they otherwise would have been. In addition, the full effects of the depreciation of the renminbi starting in 2002, which would raise exports and constrain imports, were not yet fully reflected in the trade balance. In 2005, as domestic demand in China softened somewhat and the effects of renminbi real depreciation were more fully reflected in the trade account, China's trade surplus tripled to just over $100 billion and the current account has reached $161 billion—7.2 percent of GDP.[15]

In July 2005, Chinese authorities launched a reform of the exchange rate regime that had several components: revaluing the renminbi by 2.1 percent vis-à-vis the U.S. dollar; announcing that the currency could fluctuate by up to 0.3 percent per day and that its value increasingly would be determined by supply and demand in the market; and asserting that the renminbi would be managed against a basket of currencies rather than simply being pegged to the dollar. Since that time the central bank has introduced a number of technical reforms that provide a more suitable market infrastructure for a flexible exchange regime.

As of early 2006, however, these reforms had done little to alleviate China's large and growing external imbalance. In part, this is because the initial currency revaluation of 2.1 percent was far too small. Economists Morris Goldstein and Nicholas Lardy estimated in 2003 that the extent of undervaluation on a real trade-weighted basis was in the range of 15–25 percent.[16] By the summer of 2005 the undervaluation was more likely in the range of 20–40 percent.[17]

In addition, at least through early 2006, the potential for the currency's value to move by as much as 0.3 percent per day was mostly theoretical; massive intervention continued to prevent the currency from appreciating. In the five months from July through December 2005 the authorities purchased an average of $19 billion per month in foreign exchange, almost exactly the pace of intervention that occurred in the first six months of the year. As a result, the cumulative additional appreciation of the renminbi against the dollar was only 0.8 percent. Finally, there is little evidence of pegging to a basket of currencies. China's exchange rate system remains a heavily managed peg to the dollar, and at a little changed dollar rate.[18]

China's large external imbalance poses a major risk to the global economy—and so does that of the United States. As a result of its large and growing current account deficits of recent years, the United States' international financial position has been transformed. Whereas until the mid-1980s, the United States was a net creditor country, it has now become a large net debtor. These debts now exceed one-quarter of U.S. GDP, and if the current account imbalances of recent years are not reduced to a more manageable level, U.S. net debt to the rest of the world will continue to rise. Most observers believe this path is not sustainable because the foreign appetite for holding dollar denominated assets will eventually be satiated. In addition, these large and growing U.S. external deficits are a major cause of trade protectionism in the Congress and elsewhere in the United States.

Ultimately, the adjustment of the current large external imbalances must involve a depreciation of the U.S. dollar; an improvement in the U.S. national savings/investment balance, which requires that domestic demand grow more slowly than domestic output, thus making room for expanding U.S. net exports; and a more rapid growth of domestic demand than domestic output in the rest of the world, thus leading to expanding net imports, the counterpart of expanding U.S. net exports.[19]

China has a key role in this process. As the world's second largest surplus country, China must allow its currency to appreciate against the dollar, and take steps, such as those discussed in Chapter 2, to transition to a growth path driven more by domestic consumption than by further increases in its external surplus, which is already far too large for the rest of the world to accept.

China is the prime candidate to lead in allowing its currency to appreciate for several reasons. It has a huge and rising external surplus, reflecting the substantial undervaluation of its currency. In addition, the dollar has already depreciated substantially against the world's major floating currencies, but needs to depreciate by an additional 25–30 percent in order to reduce global imbalances to a sustainable level. A substantial portion of this additional adjustment must come from Asia, where in recent years many countries, in addition to China, have intervened in the markets to prevent their currencies from appreciating, thus limiting the overall depreciation of the dollar. At least in some Asian countries, policies to avoid appreciation have been adopted because of a concern about a loss of national competitive position to China in third country markets. Thus, if China were to allow its currency to appreciate significantly it likely would lead to the desired general appreciation of Asian currencies vis-à-vis the dollar.[20]

Moreover, if China were to continue to intervene in the market, thus allowing its currency to appreciate only at the glacial pace evident since the summer of 2005, it increases the risk of stimulating a protectionist response in the United States and perhaps elsewhere.

INTELLECTUAL PROPERTY PROTECTION

China's failure to protect intellectual property (IPR) is probably the second most important source of friction in the bilateral U.S.-China economic relationship. China agreed in its WTO commitments to adhere to internationally accepted norms to protect and enforce the IPRs spelled out in the WTO Agreement on Trade-Related Aspects of Intellectual Property Rights (TRIPS). These include minimum standards of protection for copyrights, trademarks, and patents.

China has established an IPR legal regime that largely meets WTO standards. Even before it joined the WTO, the government began to amend its Patent Law, Trademark Law, and Copyright Law to make them consistent with TRIPS. Prior to entry and afterward it also issued a number of important implementing rules and regulations as well as judicial interpretations. Regulations covered protection of computer software, layout designs of integrated circuits, and so forth. The amended laws and the new regulations brought China into compliance with key IPR norms.

Enforcement of these measures has lagged substantially, however. Copyright piracy of software and recorded entertainment products continues on a wide scale, trademark counterfeiting remains rampant, and patent infringement and unauthorized use of trade secrets are widespread. The economic burden of piracy and counterfeiting falls heavily on U.S. firms, which clearly have a comparative advantage in research-based pharmaceuticals, software, movies, music, and video games.

In response to U.S. pressure, the Chinese government created a so-called IPR Leading Group in the fall of 2003 and pledged to improve enforcement action—a pledge Chinese President Hu Jintao reiterated when he met with U.S. President George W. Bush in September 2005. China also made many specific IPR enforcement commitments at the April 2004 and July 2005 meetings of the high-level Joint Commission on Commerce and Trade, notably a pledge to subject a greater range of IPR violations to criminal rather than civil penalties. (Under then-existing regulations, criminal liability thresholds were very high and evidentiary standards for criminal convictions almost impossible to meet.)

In December 2004, the Supreme People's Court and the Supreme People's Procuratorate issued a judicial interpretation reducing the monetary thresholds for criminal prosecutions of trademark and patent counterfeiting and copyright piracy.[21] Unfortunately, China does not make public sufficient information to judge the extent to which the 2004 judicial interpretation has led to a change in the enforcement of IPR laws. In October 2005 under a rarely used transparency provision of the TRIPS agreement, the United States, as well as Japan and Switzerland, requested detailed information from China on its IPR enforcement efforts over 2001–2004, as well as information on comparable cases during 2005. Unfortunately, in December 2005 the Chinese government refused to provide the information and reportedly even challenged the right of the United States to request such information.

The United States should continue to press China to fulfill its WTO IPR commitments. Whether or not this should include filing a formal complaint before the WTO Dispute Settlement Body is difficult to judge. A complaint over inadequate IPR enforcement in general is not likely to be successful because the

TRIPS agreement does not define what constitutes effective enforcement and does not require a member state to devote more resources to IPR protection than other areas of law enforcement.[22] Moreover, the ability of the U.S. Trade Representative to file a case based on inadequate enforcement in general is sometimes handicapped by the reluctance of U.S. companies to provide concrete evidence of intellectual property violations by Chinese firms.[23]

Beyond losses in China, U.S. companies increasingly suffer losses in other countries as Chinese producers of pirated and counterfeit products export their goods to the United States and third country markets. In 2004, more than 60 percent of the counterfeit goods seized in U.S. ports by Customs authorities were of Chinese origin. While the United States has for almost two decades pressured China to make increased use of criminal penalties for violators of intellectual property, the United States rarely, if ever, imposes criminal penalties on importers of counterfeit goods into its own market. Imported counterfeit and pirated goods may be seized and destroyed and the importer may face a fine, but a prison term is a rarity.

Similarly, while the United States has brought enormous pressure to bear on the Chinese government to arrest and subject to criminal penalties vendors who sell pirated and counterfeit products in Silk Alley in Beijing and similar retail locations, vendors frequently sell counterfeit and pirated products on the streets of many American cities. It should also be noted that the U.S. firm eBay operates what almost certainly is the largest marketplace in the world for counterfeit and pirated products (although it frequently deletes suspect products that are called to its attention). While some individual trademark holders, such as Tiffany, are taking advantage of the U.S. judicial system to pursue legal action against eBay, the firm has been subject to no legal action by the U.S. government. Urging the Chinese government to make more widespread use of criminal penalties against both producers and sellers of counterfeit and pirated products might yield better results if the United States led more often by example.

In any event, the United States will have to remain engaged with the Chinese on IPR issues for the foreseeable future. For one thing, many IPR violations arise or persist because of decisions of provincial and local leaders, who generally highly value the positive employment and tax contributions of factories producing pirated intellectual property. All too frequently these IPR violations appear to be concealed from the central authorities, who are more committed to enforcement of IPR laws. Thus, high-level dialogue on IPR violations, at a minimum, can provide information to the central government that might not otherwise be available.

More important, it is in the U.S. interest to ensure that rules, regulatory standards, and laws that are pending now or may be adopted in the future are consistent with or stronger than China's WTO commitments. For example, the United States should continue to encourage China to sign the Government Procurement Agreement and to accede to certain Internet protocols of the World Intellectual Property Organization (WIPO). In the realm of pending laws and regulations, the United States should seek modifications of certain provisions of a proposed anti-monopoly law, which has been in the drafting process since 1994, and a proposed regulation for national standards involving patents. Unless appropriately modified these might be used to undermine foreign companies' intellectual property rights—for example, by forcing them to license their technology at a price determined by the government. More generally, the United States should seek to persuade the Chinese to adopt market-friendly regulatory standards that provide equal market access for all firms.

While progress is likely to remain slow and the probability of using the WTO dispute settlement body successfully in IPR cases may be low, it is important to keep in mind developments that bode well for increased IPR protection in China in the long run. First, the number of patents filed and trademarks registered in China continues to increase. In 2005, China's patent applications with the WIPO soared 44 percent—pushing China, for the first time, into the ranks of the top ten patent filing countries. The long-term upward trend in trademark registrations also continued. In 1983, fewer than 20,000 trademarks were registered with the State Administration of Industry and Commerce (SAIC), the agency that manages trademarks in China. By 2004, there were 588,000 applications: the cumulative number of registered trademarks by mid-year 2005 reached 2.37 million.

Interestingly, domestic firms have registered more than 80 percent of trademarks, reflecting the strong domestic demand for this form of IPR protection. Moreover, most investigations and litigation involving trademarks and patents involve domestic firms. In the first half of 2005, for example, SAIC investigated more than 18,000 trademark infringement cases, of which only about one-eighth involved trademarks registered by foreign parties.[24] Similarly, more than 90 percent of all of the cases in China's IPR courts involve Chinese parties suing other Chinese companies for patent infringement or other IPR violations. This increasing domestic desire for IPR protection suggests China's IPR regime will improve in the years ahead.

IS CHINA BECOMING AN ADVANCED
TECHNOLOGY SUPERSTATE?

A decade or so ago, China was primarily a supplier of obviously low-tech goods, such as apparel, toys, footwear, and sporting goods, to the U.S. market. Today China is the world's largest global producer, as well as the single largest supplier to the United States, of personal computers and a broad range of seemingly much more sophisticated products. This gives rise to the concern that China is moving rapidly to dominate global markets, not just for labor-intensive manufactured goods, but also technologically more advanced products.

Is China well on the way to becoming an advanced technology superstate? The answer is crucial, since if China were able to compete globally not just at the labor-intensive end of the product spectrum but also at the capital- and technology-intensive end, it would pose a much greater competitive threat to manufacturing in the United States and other high-income countries.

Those who argue that China is emerging as a high technology

superstate examine two categories of indicators: inputs to capacity development in the fields of science and technology, including, most importantly, the training of scientific and engineering personnel and research and development (R&D) expenditures; and measures of output, particularly exports of so-called high technology products.

In terms of personnel the Chinese numbers are indeed impressive. China is currently awarding about four times as many undergraduate engineering degrees as the United States. Chinese expenditures on research and development also are rising significantly, as shown in Figure 4.7.

On the output side, there is no doubt that China has become a larger exporter of "high technology" products and that the United States is a major market for such goods. As shown in Table 4.1, based on criteria used by the Chinese government, China's global "high tech" exports in 2005 approached $220 billion and accounted for almost one-third of its total exports. That was a stunning more than 100-fold increase compared to 1989, when exports of these products were less than $2 billion and accounted for only a tiny 3.5 percent of China's total exports. The U.S. National Science Foundation's (NSF) estimates of the value of China's advanced technology exports also show explosive growth.

Estimates of bilateral trade between China and the United States in high technology products are shown in Table 4.2. The U.S. Bureau of the Census reports that the United States imported $45.7 billion in "advanced technology products" (ATP) from China in 2004, a more than sixfold increase since 1998. The American Electronics Association also tracks U.S. "tech imports" from China. Their numbers are substantially larger, showing tech imports quadrupling from $16 billion in 1998 to $68 billion in 2004.

Some analysts have utilized these data on Chinese R&D expenditures and on trade in high technology products to argue that the competitive position of the United States in advanced technology products has deteriorated sharply since 1998; that China's advanced technology industries are developing rapidly; and that China will be an advanced technology superstate by

FIGURE 4.7 China's Research and Development Expenditures, 2000–2004 (billions of $ and as a percent of GDP)

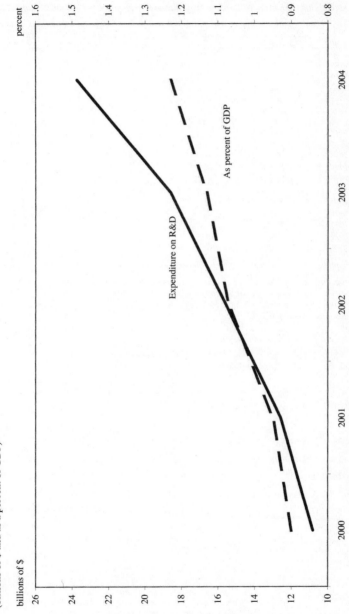

Source : National Bureau of Statistics of China, *China Statistical Yearbook 2005* (Beijing: China Statistics Press, 2005), 714; National Bureau of Statistics of China, Table of GDP at Current Prices, www.stats.gov.cn/tjdt/zygg/P020060010943108344682.doc, accessed January 9, 2006.

TABLE 4.1 China's Global Trade in High Technology Products, 1980–2005 (billions of $)

Year	Ministry of Science & Technology		National Science Foundation	
	Imports	Exports	Imports	Exports
1980	n.a	n.a	3.2	1.1
1985	n.a	n.a	16.0	1.3
1989	6.85	1.85	15.1	4.9
1990	n.a	n.a	16.0	10.1
1991	9.44	2.88	20.3	12.2
1992	10.71	4.00	28.9	17.3
1993	15.91	4.68	39.7	19.4
1994	20.60	6.34	46.5	26.4
1995	21.83	10.09	49.1	35.9
1996	22.47	12.66	54.1	44.5
1997	23.89	16.31	69.0	58.7
1998	29.20	20.25	87.1	73.4
1999	37.59	24.70	107.1	91.7
2000	52.51	37.04	151.1	132.7
2001	64.12	46.45	163.0	130.9
2002	82.86	67.86	n.a	n.a
2003	119.31	110.32	n.a	n.a
2004	161.43	165.54	n.a	n.a
2005	197.71	218.25	n.a	n.a

Source: Ministry of Science and Technology, Science and Technology Statistics, www.sts.org.cn/tjbg/jsmy/index.htm, accessed November 17, 2005; National Science Foundation, *Science and Engineering Indicators 2004* , www.nsf.gov/statistics/seind04/append/c6/at06-01.pdf, accessed November 18, 2005.

TABLE 4.2 U.S. Bilateral High Technology Trade with China, 1990–2004 (millions of $)

Year	Imports	Exports
1990	163	1,242
1991	356	1,708
1992	595	2,850
1993	1,108	3,402
1994	2,325	3,084
1995	3,456	2,471
1996	3,826	3,165
1997	4,867	3,738
1998	6,125	6,056
1999	8,217	5,007
2000	10,700	5,500
2001	13,365	7,243
2002	20,094	8,304
2003	29,345	8,290
2004	45,698	9,401

Source: U.S. Census Bureau, Foreign Trade Division, Special Tabulations as cited in National Science Foundation, *Science and Engineering Indicators 2002* , www.nsf.gov/statistics/seind02/pdf_v2.htm#c6, accessed November 18, 2005; *Science and Engineering Indicators 2006* , www.nsf.gov/statistics/seind06/append/c6/at06-06.pdf, accessed March 3, 2006.

2015.[25] These judgments are based primarily on the bilateral trade balance in high technology products. As can be calculated from the data in Table 4.2, according to the data compiled by the U.S. government, in 1998 U.S. trade with China in advanced technology products was in rough balance, but by 2004 the United States had a deficit of more than $36 billion.

On closer examination, however, the data that are used to support the hypothesis that China is rapidly emerging as a high technology superstate are flawed. On the input side, it's true that China awards four times more undergraduate engineering degrees as the United States, but only about 50 percent more master's and doctorate's degrees. Moreover, these numbers need to be scaled: A large share of China's engineering graduates are civil engineers and electrical engineers, for which there is an enormous domestic demand because of China's massive public infrastructure investment and construction boom in housing and office and retail space. China, for example, currently has about 70 to 80 major subway lines under construction, while the United States has none. Similarly China is building a massive interprovincial highway system, on a scale similar to, if not larger than, the interstate program undertaken in the United States in the 1950s.

Furthermore, while China's numbers of engineering graduates are impressive, the average quality is less so. Recent studies by the McKinsey Global Institute estimated that only one-tenth of China's engineering and IT graduates are capable of competing in the global outsourcing environment,[26] and concluded that only 160,000 of China's engineers are qualified for employment in international or high-quality domestic firms—roughly the same number available in the United Kingdom.[27]

Finally, while China's R&D expenditures are rising rapidly, they start from a very low base. China is currently spending only about one-tenth as much on R&D as the United States.[28] Indeed, the United States alone accounts for about 40 percent of global R&D expenditure, and employs almost one-third of all science and engineering researchers.[29] Some studies present data on Chinese R&D expenditures in terms of purchasing power parity, using the World Bank estimate of the purchasing power parity conversion rate for China.[30] This is a dubious procedure since it almost certainly leads to a very substantial overstatement.[31]

On the output and export side, the first key problem with the data used to support the high technology superstate hypothesis is that the definition of a high technology product varies widely. For example, the NSF estimate of China's global high technology exports for the most recent year for which data is available is about three times that published by the Chinese Ministry of Science and Technology.[32]

The problem of criteria and classification is especially obvious when one examines U.S. imports of advanced technology products. The U.S. Bureau of the Census classifies specific products as "advanced technology" if they represent "leading edge technology" in a "recognized high technology field." There are ten recognized high technology sectors, ranging from biotechnology to nuclear technology. However, 91 percent of U.S. ATP imports from China are in a single high technology sector—information and communication products. The second largest sector, optoelectronics, accounts for an additional 4 percent. U.S. imports from China are negligible in the eight other sectors, such as biotechnology, nuclear weapons, and advanced materials. Indeed, in four of the eight remaining advanced technology sectors the United States maintains a modest surplus in its trade with China.

It is not clear, however, whether the advanced technology products the U.S. imports from China in the key sectors of information and communication products and opto-electronic products should be regarded as "leading edge technology" products. For example, the largest (measured by value) ATP import from China in the information and communications category is notebook computers. In 2004, the United States imported almost 11 million notebook computers from China at an average unit cost of just over $700. The second largest value product in the sector was display units, with imports of 15 million units at an average cost of $320. Third largest was mobile phones; U.S. firms imported almost 37 million units at an average cost of about $120. The fourth largest was DVD players, of which the United

States imported 43 million at a unit cost of under $70. The largest ATP import in the opto-electronics sector is optical disc players, better known as CD players. In 2004, the United States imported more than 33 million of these from China at an average cost of less than $20 per unit. Does it make more sense for products imported in huge volumes and at relatively low cost per unit to be regarded as a "leading edge technology" or as mass-market commodities?

It is also worth noting that almost the entire growth of China's ATP exports to the United States between 1998 and 2004 is accounted for by the eightfold increase of U.S. ATP imports in the information and communications sector. For example, between 1998 and 2004 U.S. imports from China of notebook computers jumped from $5 million to $7.7 billion; display units went from $860,000 to $4.9 billion; mobile phones from $75 million to $4.3 billion; DVD players from $400,000 to $3 billion; and digital cameras from $7 million to more than $2 billion. By contrast, in most of the other sectors increases in U.S. imports from China were very modest. U.S. imports of ATP from China in the biotechnology sector, for example, increased by only a third between 1998 and 2004.

In short, on close examination the Census Bureau data on U.S. imports of advanced technology products from China hardly reflect a dramatic deterioration in U.S. competitiveness. Rather, they reflect China's emergence as the location for final assembly of a small number of very popular consumer electronic products.

Another important issue to address with respect to export data is ownership. Who owns the manufacturing facilities in China that are making so-called high technology products for the export market? And why does ownership matter?

More than half of all of China's exports and almost 90 percent of its exports of electronic and information technology products are produced by foreign-owned factories located in enclave-like settings where interaction with domestic firms appears somewhat limited.[33] Increasingly these firms are wholly foreign-owned, which makes them much less inclined than joint ventures to share technology.[34]

Notebook computers are a good example of an information technology product where the foreign share of production in China is very high. Taiwan companies currently account for 80 percent of the global output of notebook computers. Companies such as Quanta and Compal first began moving their notebook assembly operations to China only in 2001, yet rapid migration meant that by 2004, three-quarters of Taiwanese computer makers' output came from their mainland factories; in 2005, as First International Computer moved all of its notebook production to the mainland, this share rose to 90 percent. The last company with notebook computer production lines in Taiwan, Asutek Computer, announced at year-end 2005 that it would shift all of its remaining notebook production in Taiwan to China by the third quarter of 2006.[35] Taiwan companies, which do not take on local partners in their mainland operations, account for the vast majority of notebook computers exported from China.[36]

Moreover, the electronic and information technology products exported from China are largely assembled from imported parts and components. The typical notebook computer made in a Taiwanese-owned factory in China has processing chips made by Intel and an operating system made by Microsoft. Add the LCD display screens and memory chips sourced from South Korean or Taiwanese firms and hard drives sourced from Japan and almost all the value in the final product originates outside China.[37] For the processing sector as a whole, domestic value added—i.e., the cost of labor, parts, and components sourced within China, and the profits earned by foreign-owned firms in China—is only one-third of the value of output.[38] The other two-thirds is the value of imported parts and components. For electronic and information technology products exported from China, the import content is probably even higher than the average for the processing sector.

Semiconductors and microprocessors best exemplify China's dependence on imported parts and components. China has surpassed the United States and Japan to become the world's largest market for semiconductors largely because they are embedded in the electronic and information technology products that are exported in such large volumes. Imports of semiconductors and microprocessors soared from $3 billion in 1995 to more than $68 billion in 2004, when China's imports accounted for one-third of global semiconductor output of $213 billion.[39] In 2005, China's imports rose by one-third to reach $90 billion, accounting for two-fifths of global semiconductor output.[40]

Indigenous firms undoubtedly will develop the capability to produce a growing share of the high value-added parts and components that are now imported. The speed at which this capability will develop, however, is not clear. Similarly, it is difficult to judge how rapidly purely indigenous firms will develop the ability to organize large-scale production of information technology or other more advanced products. In short, evaluating the extent to which China is becoming a technological superpower involves far more than simply identifying China as the location in which seemingly more sophisticated products are assembled. One must try to understand the extent to which more advanced technologies and management techniques are diffusing into the local economy, allowing indigenous firms to accelerate their move up the technology ladder.

George J. Gilboy, a senior multinational manager based in Beijing since 1995, believes that China has not yet laid the institutional foundations that would allow it to become a technological and economic superpower. Chinese firms have failed to develop strong domestic technology supply networks; their collaboration with universities is extremely limited; and their absorption and diffusion of the technology that they import is limited.[41] Moreover, China is at the early stages of developing private property rights, respect for intellectual property, and the venture capital financing that are important long-run contributors to converting scientific and technical innovations into successful commercial ventures.

It is also important to remember that competition between companies and competition between countries are not the same thing. A technological breakthrough at a single firm may give it a substantial advantage over both foreign and domestic competitors, at least in the short run. But as a matter of policy, the United

States should welcome scientific advances in China and all other countries since ultimately advances in science abroad will contribute to further scientific progress at home.

Finally, it may be useful to recall the case of Japan. Some twenty years ago, commentators argued that the competitive edge of Japanese firms was so great and their export growth so unstoppable that Japan was likely to displace virtually all manufacturing in the United States. In retrospect, of course, this did not come to pass. U.S. firms today account for 24 percent of global manufacturing output, the same as in 1994. Japan's share has fallen from 24 percent to 21 percent in the same period, the largest decline of any advanced industrial country.[42]

DO CHINA'S PURCHASES OF U.S. BONDS CREATE VULNERABILITIES FOR THE UNITED STATES?

China has emerged in recent years as a financer of the U.S. current account deficit, which reached an all time high of about $800 billion in 2005. In both 2004 and 2005, China's purchases of foreign exchange exceeded $200 billion, reflecting its surpluses on both current account and capital account transactions, as well as large unrecorded capital inflows. On the basis of the pace of accumulation in 2004–2005, China will become the world's largest holder of official foreign exchange reserves in the second half of 2006, with the total expected to exceed one trillion U.S. dollars.[43]

A substantial portion of China's foreign exchange holdings is invested in U.S. dollar denominated bonds, such as Treasury bonds and bonds issued by Fannie Mae and Freddie Mac. Some argue that in the absence of this Chinese build-up of dollar denominated financial assets, U.S. interest rates would be much higher. This, in turn, would reduce investment in the United States, particularly in interest-sensitive sectors such as home building. The United States, in this view, is increasingly dependent on Chinese financing of its growing current account deficit. Any reduction in Chinese purchases of U.S. bonds would raise U.S. domestic interest rates and take the air out of the rising property prices in the United States. In turn, because U.S. consumption expenditures in recent years have been propped up by household spending, based on equity extracted through refinancing of increasingly expensive housing, consumption expenditures would drop.

Thus, the postulated effect of a reduction of Chinese purchases of U.S. bonds is a contraction of both investment and consumption in the United States, which could send the United States into a recession. Therefore, the argument goes, the United States should be less enthusiastic in its advice to the Chinese leadership that it significantly revalue the renminbi, since that would presumably shrink China's current account surplus, reducing Chinese purchases of U.S. bonds, raising U.S. interest rates, and slowing U.S. growth, perhaps dramatically.

Two aspects of this argument require closer examination. First, if the Chinese current account surplus fell, there would be some reduction in the size of the U.S. global current account deficit. Goldstein and Lardy estimate, for example, that if China's overall balance of payments had been in equilibrium in 2003 (i.e., a current account deficit of about 1.5 percent of GDP offsetting underlying capital inflows of 1.5 percent of GDP), the U.S. global current account deficit would have been $15 to $25 billion less than the actually recorded $540 billion.

At the time, the currencies of a number of other Asian countries were also undervalued, but these countries were reluctant to appreciate for fear of losing competitive position vis-à-vis China in third country markets. If China had allowed its currency to strengthen by 15–25 percent and the other Asian countries with fixed exchange rates had allowed similar appreciations to occur, the overall reduction in the U.S. global current account deficit would have been as much as $60–$80 billion. So if China had allowed an appreciation of its currency that had brought about the postulated overall balance of payments equilibrium, China's accumulation of foreign exchange reserves would have ended, but the need for the United States to borrow abroad to finance its trade and current account deficit would also have been smaller.

Second, a Federal Reserve study estimates that even if there had been no foreign accumulation of holdings of U.S. bonds in the twelve-month period ending in May 2005, U.S. long-term interest rates would have been only 150 basis points higher than they actually were.[44] Since China accounts for only about 15 percent of net foreign purchases of U.S. dollar denominated financial assets,[45] it appears that China's contribution to the total interest rate effect of foreign purchases of U.S. financial assets is quite small, about 20 to 25 basis points. Moreover, since the Fed has been raising interest rates over the period that China has been accumulating large U.S. dollar denominated financial assets, it is hard to argue that in the absence of Chinese purchases the U.S. economy would likely have gone into a recession sometime in the 2003–2005 time frame.

SHOULD THE UNITED STATES BE CONCERNED ABOUT CHINA'S PURCHASES OF U.S. COMPANIES?

Finally, how concerned should the United States be about the purchase of U.S. assets by Chinese companies, such as Lenovo's purchase of the IBM PC business or proposed but subsequently withdrawn offers, such as Haier's bid for Maytag and the China National Offshore Oil Corporation's (CNOOC) bid for Unocal, all of which occurred in 2005? How large are transactions of this type? Do any represent a threat to U.S. national security, and if so, how? Do they give China control of critical defense technologies or supplies of high technology goods or resources that could enhance China's military capabilities in the event of a military conflict with the United States? Or is the primary threat to U.S. economic interests rather than national security? And if so, should the Exon-Florio Bill, which provides for the review of potential foreign acquisition of U.S. companies by an interagency committee led by the Department of the Treasury, be amended?

It is important to note at the outset that Chinese firms until quite recently have been extremely modest foreign direct investors. In the three-year period 2002–2004, annual net direct investment by Chinese firms abroad averaged only $1.4 billion and accounted for only 0.3 percent of global foreign direct investment outflows.[46] Investment by Chinese firms in the United States has been a small fraction of these global outflows. According to U.S. government data, Chinese net direct investment in the United States in the five-year period 2000 through 2004 averaged less than $50 million annually and accounted for only 0.01 percent of inward direct investment from all countries. On a stock basis, China's investment position in the United States is also very low. At year-end 2004, Chinese firms' cumulative foreign direct investment in the United States (valued on a historical cost basis) was less than $500 million and accounted for only 0.03 percent of cumulative inward direct investment.

In short, China is not even remotely near the point that Japan occupied in the late 1980s and early 1990s, at the peak of its direct investments in the United States. In the five-year period 1987–1991, average annual Japanese direct investment into the United States exceeded $15 billion, 300 times recent Chinese inflows. Japan alone accounted for one-third of all foreign direct investment inflows into the United States in 1987–1991, many, many times China's miniscule share of recent years. By the end of 1991, Japan's direct investment position in the United States was almost $13 billion, twenty-five times China's position at year-end 2004.[47]

However, foreign investment by Chinese firms is likely to grow significantly on a global basis in the years ahead. In large part this is because Chinese government policy now encourages its three major international oil companies "to build up secure supplies abroad through purchasing equity shares in overseas markets, exploring and drilling abroad, constructing refineries, and building pipelines to Siberia and Central Asia."[48]

Meanwhile, many Chinese low-cost manufacturers aspire to move from contract manufacturing for established global companies to direct sales of their own global brands. More of these firms are likely to follow the example of Lenovo's purchase of the IBM PC business and TCL's acquisition of the television business of the French electronics company Thomson SA. In each of these cases the Chinese firms sought the brand and marketing channels of the foreign firm, which when combined with China's indigenous manufacturing prowess was thought to provide a shortcut to vastly expanded global sales. As a result, Chinese net foreign direct investment outflows jumped to $3.9 billion in the first half of 2005, more than five times the average pace of purchases in the previous three years.

Judging from the Chinese acquisitions that have been made over the past year this number is likely to rise further—especially since the Chinese government announced in early 2006 that it planned to abolish the annual foreign exchange quota limiting outbound foreign direct investment. It is therefore instructive to review some of the issues raised by CNOOC's proposed acquisition of Unocal in 2005.

Critics of CNOOC's bid for Unocal charged that the transaction would make the United States more dependent on foreign oil and thus harm U.S. interests. This charge reflects a fundamental misunderstanding of the global oil market. Had China acquired Unocal and diverted its entire output to China, its net effect on the United States and the global oil market would have been negligible. For every barrel of oil China imported from Unocal fields, it would import a barrel less from other sources, so the net effect on the global oil market would be nil. China's key impact on the global market for energy is the pace of its domestic growth and the efficiency with which it uses energy. These are the two key variables that will determine China's influence on the global price of oil, not whether China purchases its oil on the global spot market, acquires it through long-term supply contracts, or acquires it through foreign fields that it owns outright or in which it has a smaller equity stake.

More broadly, the supposition that fundamental U.S. and Chinese interests diverge on global energy issues is profoundly incorrect. Both the United States and China are large net oil importers and thus share an interest in a stable Middle East, increased global investment in oil production, and the development of economically viable alternative energy technologies. China's ownership of foreign oil and gas assets need not adversely affect U.S. interests. As already noted, in the short run the diversion of the output of these fields to China would have a negligible effect on global energy availability and prices. And in the long run, given China's interest in lower cost energy, Chinese firms are likely to invest at least as much as alternative owners in expanding oil and gas production in foreign locations, which, of course, benefits the United States and all other energy importing countries.

In the short run, of course, there is an important divergence of interests as China invests in oil and gas development in Iran and Sudan and thwarts U.S. efforts to impose economic sanctions on both countries. But, as suggested by Flynt Leverett and Jeff Bader of the Brookings Institution, these short-term challenges need to be managed so that the two countries can work together to meet their common energy objectives. The United States for its part should reject special review arrangements of proposed Chinese purchases of U.S. oil and gas assets, such as those voted by Congress when the CNOOC acquisition was pending. The U.S. government has long encouraged other countries to adopt open investment policies that promote the free cross-border flow of capital, among other reasons to insure access for U.S. firms to invest abroad in energy production. Imposing a special review requirement only on investments by Chinese firms, beyond the normal review of the Committee on Foreign Investment in the United States (CFIUS), which has applied to all foreign acquisitions of U.S. assets since 1975, runs counter to this long run goal and thus is ill advised.

Similarly, the terms of the CFIUS review of foreign acquisitions should not be expanded to go beyond the long-standing national security criterion: Economic nationalism or, even worse, thinly disguised racism should not be a factor in CFIUS reviews. Finally, as suggested by Leverett and Bader, the United States should "take the lead in encouraging and facilitating Chinese membership in the IEA (International Energy Agency)."[49]

HOW SHOULD CHINA'S ROLE IN THE
GLOBAL ECONOMIC SYSTEM EVOLVE?

China's trade growth has dramatically accelerated since it joined the WTO in late 2001. Less noticed is that in the last few years, China has initiated discussions with 27 countries and regions to form bilateral and regional free trade agreements (FTAs). Bilateral negotiations include those with Australia and New Zealand, while the most important regional discussions are with the Association of Southeast Asian Nations (ASEAN). Discussions with ASEAN starting in 2002 led to the November 2004 signing of the Agreement on Trade in Goods of the Framework Agreement for Overall Economic Cooperation, the first step toward formation of an ASEAN-China free trade area (ACFTA) by 2010. The first cuts in tariffs on industrial goods, covering more than 7,000 products, took effect on July 1, 2005. Parallel agreements on trade in services and on investment are expected to follow.

None of these agreements and negotiations involves the United States, raising concerns that the United States will suffer from significant trade diversion. Trade diversion arises when one country, which has a higher cost of producing a good, is able to use preferred market access to take market share away from another country with lower production costs. For example, if Japan and China negotiate a bilateral FTA, Japanese firms, by virtue of the lower tariffs they gain in China, may be able to take market share from U.S. firms for some products. Trade diversion would occur when Japan's preferential tariff more than compensates for its higher production costs.

The threat of trade diversion for the United States from China's FTAs appears modest in the aggregate, but could be significant for the most affected sectors.[50] Losses to the United States will take some time to appear since tariff reductions in ACFTA will be phased in and remain incomplete. For example, while the initial tariff reductions cover a large number of products, the share for which tariffs have been cut to zero is initially quite small, under 5 percent in 2005. Moreover, even when the agreement is fully phased in (in 2010 for trade between China and the six original

ASEAN members—Brunei, Indonesia, Malaysia, the Philippines, Singapore, and Thailand; in 2015 for trade between China and the newer members of ASEAN—Burma, Cambodia, Laos, and Vietnam), tariffs will not go to zero on all products. As in the ASEAN Free Trade Agreement, each ACFTA member has reserved the right to designate sensitive products for which the tariff reduction process is slower and in the end incomplete.[51]

In the long run, the best U.S. defense against trade diversion is the completion of the Doha round of trade liberalization and concluding bilateral FTAs with the same countries. If more progress is made in reducing tariff and other barriers on a multilateral basis, trade diversion created by bilateral or regional FTAs is less. U.S. bilateral FTAs with more countries in the region would eliminate the possibility of diversion arising with respect to those countries. In any case, since the United States has signed the North American and Central American FTAs and other FTAs and is pursuing additional agreements, including with Korea and Thailand, it has little basis for complaining about China's preferential trade agreements.

On the other hand, because China is such a large global trading country, the United States and other members of the WTO can reasonably expect that China play an important role in bringing the Doha Round of multilateral trade negotiations to a successful conclusion. China has gained substantially from participating in the global trading system. Rather than arguing that its commitments to enter the WTO were so far-reaching that it should not be expected to offer more access to its market, it should be making positive offers for liberalization that would contribute to a successful conclusion of the Doha Round—all the more so because a Doha failure likely would lead to backsliding on market opening in China's biggest markets (the United States and the European Union) with potential large adverse effects on the Chinese economy.

China's role in the global economic system ranges far beyond its participation in the WTO and the Doha negotiations. China has been a member of the IMF and the World Bank since 1980 and greatly values its participation in these institutions, for both their substantive contributions to their own economic objectives and the status that membership brings.

A central issue is how to further integrate China, the rapidly emerging economic superpower, into the existing system of global economic governance. Historically, integrating newly rising economic powers in the global leadership structure has been difficult—but failing to do so for China could impair the prospects for constructive Chinese participation in international economic cooperation, thereby exacerbating the risks posed by its rapid rise.

Most importantly, what role will China play in the evolution of informal global institutions that provide overarching international economic policy coordination? Many possibilities exist, ranging from including China in the G-7; elevating the G-20 to the key international economic steering committee, which already includes China and with which China may feel more comfortable because of the membership of other developing countries; or creating a G-4 that would include only the United States, the European Union, Japan, and China, clearly the most important players in the world economy.[52] These possibilities, and perhaps others, should be explored with a view to identifying the arrangements that are most likely to encourage China to play the role of a responsible stakeholder in global economic issues.

On balance China's economic rise creates an opportunity for the United States and the global economy more broadly. Because of the large size of its economy, its rapid growth, and its remarkable openness, China has emerged as a major source of global economic growth. The annual gains to the United States from increasing economic interaction with China are substantial—about $70 billion or $625 per household.[53] The large and growing U.S. deficit in its trade with China largely reflects the relocation of labor-intensive assembly activities to China from elsewhere in Asia, rather than a Chinese policy of restricting access to its domestic market. The assertion that China already is moving rapidly up the technology ladder and thus soon will displace U.S.

workers involved in more skilled and capital-intensive production does not seem to be supported by a careful analysis of China's training of technical and engineering personnel, expenditures on research and development, or changing mix of exports.

China's economic rise, however, creates important distributional consequences in the United States and elsewhere. Since China exports primarily labor-intensive goods and imports more capital-intensive goods, its growing global economic footprint tends to put downward pressure on the wages of less skilled workers while raising both the wages of more skilled workers and returns to capital. China thus underscores the need for the United States to develop effective programs of transitional assistance and education and training to assist those workers who have lost jobs or moved to lower paying jobs as a result of trade expansion.

Moreover, China's exchange rate policy in the last few years and its failure to provide adequate protection to intellectual property pose additional challenges for the United States. China's undervalued currency is an obstacle to the reduction of global economic imbalances and its weak IPR regime imposes significant costs on U.S. firms. Absent improvement on these fronts China risks setting off a protectionist reaction in the United States and undermines the prospect of China assuming a greater role in the global economic governance system.

5

China's Foreign and
Security Policy:
Partner or Rival?

Rather than offering an explicit outline of a long-term national security strategy, China often characterizes its foreign policy and national security goals in terms of a series of principles and slogans. Since the 1980s under Deng Xiaoping, Beijing has said it pursues an "independent foreign policy of peace." Under this rubric, China's fundamental foreign policy goals, as outlined in official public documents, are "to preserve China's independence, sovereignty and territorial integrity" and to "create a favorable international environment for China's reform and opening up and modernization."[1] There is little reason to doubt that these goals reflect China's actual priorities, at least in the near term, as they reflect the legacy of China's difficult modern history.

China often cites its "century of humiliation"—when foreign powers divided and subjugated China beginning in the middle of the nineteenth century until the end of World War II—as a touchstone for its explicit commitment to preserving China's independence, sovereignty, and territorial integrity. In fact, Chinese Imperial history dating back two millennia is filled with examples of national division, vulnerability to "foreign" aggression, and violations of Han Chinese sovereignty. Chinese "unity" as a result is equated in China's national consciousness with the height of the country's power and prestige, while division and disunity are associated with its lowest points of weakness and humiliation.

This historical memory may also be shaping the Chinese Communist Party (CCP) leadership's international outlook and policy. The popular demonstrations that engulfed China in the spring of 1989, and which ended with tanks in Tiananmen Square, convinced China's leaders that enhancing the Party's popular standing and legitimacy depended on delivering practical and psychological benefits for the Chinese people. As communism declined as a credible and unifying ideology, boosting China's prosperity, restoring its prestige and stature as a great power, and unifying the nation—that is, returning Hong Kong, Macao, and Taiwan to the "motherland"—became critical measures of the CCP's fitness to lead and, arguably, essential elements of regime survival itself.

Today, having recovered Hong Kong and Macao, China's concern over its "territorial integrity" is most associated with (re)assumption of sovereign control over Taiwan and continued control over the restive western autonomous regions of Xinjiang and Tibet. Japan colonized Taiwan after the 1895 Sino-Japanese War, and China considers Taiwan's continued separation from the mainland a lingering legacy of its "century of humiliation." The Taiwan issue remains the one national consideration that influences Chinese foreign policy in a consistent and fundamental way. Beijing demands acceptance of the "One China" principle as a precondition to establishing diplomatic relations with another country, and will sacrifice other interests, including aspects of its international reputation, in order to isolate Taiwan internationally in a strategy to prevent permanent separation, and perhaps compel unification, over time.

Beijing has mimicked Taiwan's traditional "money diplomacy" to draw official recognition from the dwindling number of African, Latin American, and Oceanic nations that have official diplomatic relations with the Republic of China on Taiwan. The Republic of Macedonia learned the hard way the cost of crossing Beijing on Taiwan: After Skopje established diplomatic relations with Taipei in the 1990s, China used its veto power in the United Nations Security Council to block passage of a peacekeeping bill to aid Macedonia. At the UN General Assembly in September 2005, President Hu offered debt forgiveness and duty-free entry to exports from the world's poor countries—except for those countries that recognize Taipei.

China's other strategic goal, to promote an "international environment for China's reform and opening up and modernization," is consistent with Beijing's turn in late 1978 away from radical leftist ideology toward a more pragmatic orientation that placed priority on raising the living standards of the Chinese people and building up China's comprehensive national power through economic development. China has proclaimed its interest in a "peaceful international environment" to enable Beijing to focus its energies on its enormous internal challenges. This has meant China has put a premium on maintaining positive and benign international relationships, particularly with nations that will have an impact on its domestic stability and national development.

In recent years, China has placed particular emphasis on the development of a "good-neighborly relationship and partnership"[2] with border countries—with a focus on preventing external threats from exacerbating internal frictions in China, or threatening China's well-being, stability, and territorial integrity. China's relations with Central, South, and Southeast Asia, and even the Middle East, reflect Beijing's concern over cross-border influence into its western-most ethnic minority regions, particularly Xinjiang. China wants to prevent encouragement of "separatism," prevent the formation of anti-China blocs that may constrain China's freedom of action or contain its development, and preempt developments that may threaten or challenge China's sense of security along its extensive land and maritime border.

In this effort, China has emphasized non-military aspects of its comprehensive national power, adopting a three-pronged approach of setting aside areas of disagreement with neighboring states, focusing on confidence-building measures to promote ties, and engaging in economic integration and multilateral cooperation to address shared concerns. China has settled most of its border disputes, and otherwise met with much success in its efforts to place relations with neighbors on a positive footing. Nonetheless, many problems persist, including several territorial disputes—most notably with India over Aksai Chin and Arunachel Pradesh, with Japan over the Diaoyutai/Senkaku islands and the demarcation of the East China Sea, and with four Southeast Asian countries over the Paracel and Spratly islands in the South China Sea.

While the region is heartened by China's attempts to demonstrate its humility and commitment to mutual economic benefit, a layer of uncertainty remains among many in East Asia about the future foreign policy implications of China's rise. Commitment to "territorial integrity" and "good-neighborly relations," in fact, can work at cross-purposes. Although China says it is not interested in territorial expansion, continued territorial disputes involving China beg the questions, What is Chinese territory? How will overlapping claims be resolved? The answers may have a measurable impact on the future strategic outlines of East Asia, and serve as important markers for how China intends to handle dispute resolution in general as its power grows.

The final specific motivating factor underlying Chinese foreign policy today concerns China's urgent need to acquire the natural resources, including but not limited to energy (oil and natural gas), necessary to fuel its economic development. Beijing has reached out assertively to virtually all nations with resources available for export to help keep China's economic machine running. This often has led to close Chinese relationships with unsavory regimes.

China has promoted its "peaceful development/rise" campaign to reassure the world that it will pursue a different development path than did Germany and Japan in the late nineteenth and early twentieth centuries—a path based not on aggressive changes to the international order, but instead on benevolent principles of mutual benefit. Chinese leaders explicitly state China's lack of interest in regional hegemony or international leadership (perhaps except in the context of promoting the interests of the developing world). Whether China's future strategists will share this vision, however, remains necessarily unknowable, even to Beijing's current leadership.

HOW DOES CHINA VIEW
THE UNITED STATES?

China recognizes the "unipolar" environment in which the United States exercises enormous political, economic, and military power and influence internationally, including in Asia. The vast U.S. market remains critical for the success of China's developmental transition. Given Beijing's paramount near- and mid-term priority on attending to its internal challenges and maintaining a peaceful international environment, China places enormous value on maintaining a positive relationship with the United States. Chinese leaders know they can ill-afford to make an enemy of the United States, at least for the foreseeable future.

Nonetheless, among the Chinese elite and masses, positive and negative images of the United States intermingle to create a complex mindset.[3] China's people remain enamored of U.S. wealth, power, freedoms, advanced technology, and popular culture, and feel positively about Americans as individuals. At the same time, they are suspicious of and attuned to perceived hypocrisy in U.S. foreign policy. Elite Chinese harbor lingering grievances over past indignities and perceived victimization at the hands of the United States—including the EP-3 spy plane incident in 2001, the accidental U.S. bombing of China's embassy in Belgrade in 1999, U.S. congressional opposition in the mid-1990s to China's application to host the Olympic Games, and continuing U.S. arms sales and defense support for Taiwan, among other examples—with uncertain long-term implications for the relationship, particularly given rising populist nationalism in China.

In recent years, China's leaders have assiduously sought to maintain a relationship with Washington that is correct and cordial, if not conspicuously warm. Beijing is satisfied with the George W. Bush Administration's current mantra that it pursues "candid, cooperative, and constructive" relations with China, and Beijing endorses the U.S. approach of highlighting publicly areas of mutual interest while managing differences quietly. Washington's theme of encouraging China to be a "responsible stakeholder" in international affairs is generally seen as a constructive effort to build a positive and sustainable framework for the bilateral relationship, although there are muted concerns in some corners that accepting the concept may force Beijing to give up its foreign policy of "independence" to join the United States in an international system that is viewed as predominantly serving U.S. interests.

The two countries maintain many avenues of cooperation, and in recent years have increased government, military, and people-to-people exchanges in the fields of counterterrorism, nonproliferation, UN reform, health, energy, and the environment. The United States now maintains an FBI office in Beijing. U.S.-China cooperation has also increased through multilateral forums such as the ASEAN (Association of Southeast Asian Nations) Regional Forum and APEC (the Asia Pacific Economic Cooperation forum), and the two countries have worked closely to coordinate the organization and conduct of Six Party talks to eliminate North Korea's nuclear weapons program. The initiation of a semi-annual U.S.-China vice-ministerial Senior Dialogue on strategic issues also is a positive step to facilitate candid communication, build understanding, prevent miscalculation, and exchange perspectives at a senior level.

Nevertheless, in its public language and policies, China often reveals its discomfort with U.S. global predominance. Beijing commonly proclaims its opposition to "hegemony and power politics," code words for U.S. foreign policy that gained rhetorical currency during the 1990s (although originally used during the Cold War to connote the Soviet Union).

Beijing's primary worry about the United States, however, concerns overall U.S. intentions toward China and U.S. foreign policy in China's neighborhood. Many Chinese officials and elite are convinced that the United States will seek to slow or block China's emergence as a great power—whether by permanently separating Taiwan from the mainland, de facto if not de jure; depriving China of an adequate supply of energy for its development; or inducing change in China's political system. Indeed, Chinese internal documents commonly refer to suspicions that the United States seeks to "split (*fenhua*) and Westernize (*xihua*)" China.

It is through such a prism that China views U.S. interests such as humanitarian intervention, preemption, alliances, and even missile defense. Each of these matters is connected, for instance, to potential U.S. defense of Taiwan (*fenhua*). When the United States talks of propagating "universal values" of democracy and human rights worldwide, Beijing sees *xihua*—or U.S. intent to reshape China in its own image, induce the downfall of the Chinese Communist Party, and exercise greater power and control in Chinese affairs.

Chinese leaders are particularly attuned to the lessons of the Cold War. Many suspect the United States seeks to draw China down the same path it led the Soviet Union, leading to the collapse and dissolution of the Chinese state. China often acts consciously to avoid mirroring Soviet missteps, whether by abjuring the notion of engaging in an arms race with the United States, carefully affirming its intent not to place itself in ideological opposition to the United States, or focusing on economic development before addressing dramatic political reform.

Beijing's concern extends to U.S. influence along China's periphery, in particular the potential for development of anti-China blocs led by the United States (or others) that may seek to contain Chinese power or infiltrate and destabilize China's minority regions. Beijing has even betrayed some nervousness over the influence of U.S. nongovernmental organizations (NGOs) operating in former Soviet republics, where populist "color revolutions" in recent years have led to the overthrow of autocratic regimes, in some cases along China's border. China's leaders remain suspicious that word of such movements may reach restive peoples within China, or that China may otherwise become subject to such movements, particularly as domestic turmoil and transition intensify.

Beijing was quietly relieved after September 11, 2001, when the immediate threat of *jihadist* terrorism pushed the U.S. spotlight away from China. Anything that distracted the United States and enabled China to focus on its urgent domestic challenges was welcomed. Beijing's pronouncement in 2002 of a two-decade "period of strategic opportunity" for China was related to this post-9/11 calculation. Nonetheless, Chinese leaders remain worried that once the United States is no longer preoccupied with terrorism, Washington will return its attention to the "China threat."

China recognizes the reality of a U.S.-dominated world for the foreseeable future, and will likely accommodate where its vital national interests are not directly at stake. China, for instance, supported U.S. actions in Afghanistan following September 11, and remained relatively quiet about other U.S. actions in the war on terrorism, content to let others take the lead. In contrast to its aggressive criticism of the U.S. intervention in Kosovo in the late 1990s, China has not loudly condemned the United States for the war in Iraq. However, Chinese strategists consider the United States China's likely foremost strategic rival over the long term.

IS CHINA TRYING TO PUSH THE UNITED STATES OUT OF EAST ASIA?

Some U.S. observers suspect that China's strategic ambition is to push the United States out of East Asia and become the dominant regional hegemon, akin to the Sino-centric order of China's imperial period. Chinese leaders deny such an ambition, and try to reassure U.S. audiences in public and private that they do not seek to evict or supplant the United States in the region, either militarily or politically. Nonetheless, suspicions about China's real feelings and intentions persist.

For example, Chinese leaders express neither open opposition nor active support (as other regional nations do) for the U.S. presence in East Asia. Instead, China tends publicly to "respect" or acknowledge the reality of U.S. presence, which suggests, at best, tolerance of the situation.

At the same time, China's 2002 Defense White Paper called U.S. efforts to strengthen its military alliances in Asia one of the "factors of instability" in the region.[4] China's repeatedly stated opposition to a "Cold War mentality" and to "hegemony and power politics" in international affairs are also semi-oblique references to its concerns about U.S foreign policy and influence in East Asia (and beyond). Since the 1990s, China has promoted a "New Security Concept" that dubs U.S. alliances and military presence Cold War "relics," and affirms Beijing's opposition in principle to "military blocs" and "military alliances," thinly veiled references to the U.S. security structure in East Asia and to the basing of U.S. military forces in Japan, South Korea, and more recently, Central Asia. The concept promotes confidence-building measures and informal "strategic partnerships" as alternatives.

Because the rest of East Asia continues to support the U.S.-centered regional security structure, China has downplayed its concerns in recent years. However, Beijing has been central to the development of multilateral vehicles to promote regional identity that do not involve the United States. In each case, China claims that it was not the driving force behind the initiatives, but rather followed the desires of smaller regional powers in ASEAN and Central Asia. The Shanghai Cooperation Organization (SCO), made up of Kazakhstan, Kyrgyzstan, Tajikistan, Uzbekistan, Russia, and China, for instance, originally was established to settle border disputes but has now become an active vehicle for regional cooperation to tackle the "three evils" of "terrorism, religious extremism, and separatism," and perhaps hedge against undesirable U.S. influence. China's behind-the-scenes efforts have been critical to the creation and evolving agenda of these organizations.

Chinese leaders also call the SCO and ASEAN + 3 (China, Japan, and Korea) dialogues examples of China's new security concept in action. Some analysts suspect that, having failed to convince the region of the benefits of its new security concept over the traditional U.S.-centered security structure, China has decided to push ahead with its vision in a longer-range attempt to dilute, if not undermine, U.S. regional influence.

Some Chinese analysts will assert that Beijing's primary concern about U.S. presence in East Asia relates specifically to U.S. assistance to Taiwan. They argue that absent the Taiwan problem, Beijing would have no problem with the United States in Asia. Taiwan in fact is a major factor in China's concern over U.S. regional force presence. Nonetheless, it is unlikely that Taiwan alone accounts for China's discomfort with U.S. presence. As stated, China remains suspicious that the United States seeks to contain China's development more broadly, and continuation of U.S. alliances and force presence as the dominant features of East Asian security will likely remain uncomfortable for an increasingly powerful and proud China.

Nonetheless, Beijing is becoming more confident that trends in national power are moving in its favor. China has leveraged the obvious power of an economically vibrant and growing nation of more than a billion people to ensure that its interests are met with due respect by regional states, without accentuating its growing military power (although the region is clearly aware of this development). Under such conditions, China need not explicitly affirm its desire for regional predominance to achieve this result over time.

Likewise, seeking regional hegemony or directly challenging the United States for regional leadership would unnecessarily distract and divert China's attention from its more critical domestic needs. The Chinese Communist Party has learned the lesson of the Soviet Union's fall: It knows its hold on power depends not on rivalry with the United States or excessive international engagements or ideological considerations, but on whether it can deliver public goods to its people. Consequently, aside from the issue of Taiwan, Beijing may indeed recognize the benefits of U.S.-based regional security, at least at present.

The region will likely continue to support a U.S. presence to serve at least as a tacit counterbalance, or hedge, against the uncertain trajectory of Chinese power. To assist the region in its future strategic calculations, however, the United States will also need to consider how to integrate Beijing more fully into the alliance-centered regional security structure—from which China is currently excluded, and of which Beijing views itself as the primary target.

IS CHINA ENGAGED IN
GLOBAL STRATEGIC COMPETITION
WITH THE UNITED STATES?

China rejects any suggestion of global strategic competition with the United States. Nonetheless, China has become notably more proactive in its economic and diplomatic outreach to build constructive bilateral ties with an increasing array of nations. The focus of China's increasing global attention is primarily economic, to acquire the resources, secure the investments, and engage the markets China will need to continue its remarkable economic growth, safeguard domestic stability, and develop its comprehensive national power.

At the same time, China's more proactive outreach is also consistent with longer-term political goals. China has promoted the notion of a "multipolar world" in which several pillars of global power, including China, would balance U.S. global influence. Beijing has concluded that, given the level of U.S. predominance, this multipolarity will not be achieved in the near term; nonetheless, Chinese strategists clearly aspire to this goal over time, and China's international actions may be considered in this context. Beijing has made special efforts to resolve disputes and promote ties with historic rivals such as India and Russia, both of which share China's call for a multipolar world.

In an attempt to reassure the international community about its own peaceful nature and to implicitly distinguish itself from the United States, Beijing's foreign policy statements and documents repeatedly affirm China's adherence to principles of peace, openness, development, equality and democracy among nations, cooperation, dialogue, consultation, justice, and win-win results. In this way, China is able not only to take the high ground in international discourse but also to place others, including the United

States, on the defensive, and hamstring any incentive or attempts to bandwagon against growing Chinese power.[5]

China's outreach to the developing world is of particular interest in this regard. Despite China's substantial economic achievements over the past 25 years, China still refers to itself as the "world's largest developing country." Beijing's official documents refer specifically to the developing world as a critical component of Chinese foreign policy goals to promote a multipolar world and "democratized international relations."

China's interest in the developing world extends back to the Cold War, when Beijing assumed for itself ideological leadership over the revolutionary agenda of insurgents in Africa, Latin America, and elsewhere. Today, China's ideological emphasis is gone, but its desire to lead in promoting the collective interests of the South has endured. China's promotion of equality and democracy in international affairs, opposition to external intervention in internal affairs, and support overall for the "Five Principles of Peaceful Coexistence"[6] provide a sense of kinship with developing world leaders, and offer a competing vision to Washington's example.

China's involvement in a variety of international dialogues[7] and bilateral aid programs[8] has also sought to demonstrate its commitment to partnership with the developing world. China, with Brazil and India, for instance, has used the Doha negotiations of the World Trade Organization (WTO) to urge the United States and EU to liberalize their agriculture and industrial markets. Nonetheless, Beijing's record in international institutions and forums such as the United Nations and WTO is spotty, and suggests that Chinese self-interest will often win out over notions of "South-South" solidarity, a fact recognized by many in the developing world.

China's Energy Diplomacy

China's need for an uninterrupted and secure supply of natural resources, particularly energy (oil and natural gas), has become an increasingly important strategic element of Beijing's international relations.

Over the last decade, China's share of the world's energy consumption has risen from 9 to 12 percent.[9] China continues to rely on the Middle East for almost half of its oil imports, although in recent years, Beijing has sought to diversify China's sources of energy supply—particularly through gaining control of energy production assets or acquiring stakes in overseas energy companies (see Table 5.1). The difficulties Chinese companies have had in acquiring mainstream energy companies, such as the controversial bid by CNOOC (China National Offshore Oil Corporation) for Unocal in 2005, have fueled China's search for energy assets in such countries as Iran, Burma, Angola, and Sudan. In the process, China's natural resource/energy diplomacy has helped create ties with nations throughout the world that may serve as the basis for broader cooperation.

With 90 percent of China's imported oil transported by oceangoing tanker,[10] China's energy diplomacy also has implications for its naval and maritime policy. Beijing's attempt to bypass potential chokepoints such as the Strait of Malacca, through which 80 percent of China's oil imports transit, has spurred the development of port facilities at Gwadar in Pakistan, and in Bangladesh and Burma.[11] Aside from the risk of collisions, piracy, and terrorist attacks, China's oil tankers are dependent on the U.S. Navy to patrol and secure these sea lanes, which China views as a strategic vulnerability should U.S.-China relations turn sour. China will likely seek to overcome this vulnerability by playing a more proactive role in securing its energy supply, perhaps by expanding its blue water naval capabilities and by developing more overland pipelines extending from South, Southeast, Central, and Northeast Asia. Such responses would affect its strategic relationships throughout the region, and, absent greater strategic cooperation and careful management of the energy issue, potentially lead to further rivalry and suspicion in its relations with the United States.

TABLE 5.1 China's Oil Imports by Region (percent)

Region	1990[i]	1997[ii]	2001[iii]	2004[iv]
Asia Pacific	60.6	26.2	14	11.5
Middle East	39.4	47.5	56	45.4
Africa	0	16.7	23	28.7
Other (Europe, Americas)	0	9.6	7	14.3

[i] *Source*: International Energy Agency, *China's Worldwide Quest for Energy Security*, 2000, 50.

[ii] *Source*: Ibid.

[iii] *Source*: U.S.-China Economic and Security Review Commission, *2004 Report to Congress of the U.S.-China Economic and Security Review Commission* (Washington, DC: U.S. Government Printing Office, June 2004), 156.

[iv] *Source*: China OGP (Oil, Gas and Petroleum) Newsletter (2005), *Xinhua News Agency*.

Strategic Opportunism?

China's proactive global outreach in recent years is natural for a growing nation of China's size and stature, particularly one with substantial economic needs and a desire to demonstrate its constructive and peaceful intent. At the same time, U.S. observers have detected a degree of strategic opportunism in China's foreign relations in recent years relative to the United States.

In May 2005, for example, Beijing hosted Uzbek President Islam Karimov only two weeks after the United States condemned him for violently suppressing unrest in the Uzbek city of Andijan. Shortly thereafter, President Karimov ordered the United States to withdraw its military presence from the Karshi-Khanabad (K2) base within six months, and in July 2005, the Shanghai Cooperation Organization issued a statement calling on the United States to set a timetable for withdrawing its entire military presence from

Central Asia. While China may not have initiated these moves, Beijing (and Moscow) clearly did not object, suggesting China may have deemed the threat of a long-term U.S. military presence on its western periphery of greater strategic importance than U.S. counterterrorism efforts in South Asia.

In 2003, Beijing took advantage of a period of particular tension between the United States and the Philippines to reach agreements with the Philippine government on closer political, military-to-military, and intelligence ties (although implementation has proved slow). In September 2002, Beijing appointed a Middle East peace envoy to help with the Israel-Palestinian impasse, a curious undertaking that did not have a measurable impact but which seemed to highlight the lack of effective U.S. diplomatic engagement in the matter at the time, and served as a confidence-building measure to represent China's goodwill and interest in engaging as a responsible international actor.

Likewise, China has leveraged growing trade relations with Latin American countries, and the desire of many Latin governments to demonstrate their political independence from the United States, to enhance its political ties with Argentina, Bolivia, Brazil, and Chile. Meanwhile, U.S. decisions to sanction and/or isolate regimes in Cuba, Venezuela, Sudan, Burma, Angola, and elsewhere have provided an economic opportunity for Chinese investors, traders, and energy companies to fill the gap. In the process, political relationships with these pariah nations have developed to varying degrees to offer China (and these nations) at least a short-term strategic opportunity in relation to the United States.

In the wake of tensions between the United States and Europe during the first term of the George W. Bush administration, China attempted, less successfully, to leverage its growing relationship with the European Union to exploit transatlantic differences. The EU and China have a robust economic, social, and political relationship: The EU is now China's largest trading partner;[12] twice as many Chinese students are studying in European universities as in U.S. institutions; and Brussels and Beijing have established an annual dialogue at multiple levels that is reinforced by bilateral summits between individual European nations and China. In 2005, the EU considered lifting its Tiananmen Square–era arms embargo on China, but strong U.S. opposition, combined with China's promulgation of the Anti-Secession Law (against Taiwan), derailed the effort—at least for the time being. In the end, Europe's strong aversion to China's human rights record, new transatlantic dialogues concerning China, and the gradual mending of transatlantic ties have helped to better harmonize U.S. and EU perspectives on China.

Southeast Asia

China's relations with Southeast Asia have garnered particular notice among U.S. strategists in recent years. Beijing has already established itself as a significant political player to rival the United States. China's help to the region during the 1997–98 financial crisis established new credibility for Beijing, especially in light of Washington's initial unresponsiveness. China has tied itself closer to the region through expanded trade, investment, transportation, and other cooperative ties; promotion of a regional free trade agreement; and conclusion of energy supply pacts. Beijing has also demonstrated its commitment to the region's ethos, paying due respect to the "ASEAN way" of confidence-building and consensus, and to multilateral dialogues to address transnational issues. China generally has done a very effective job in recent years in changing the perspective of Southeast Asian nations toward viewing China's emergence as a net benefit rather than a threat, particularly on the economic front.

At the same time, China has sought to build a sense of community within the region, often excluding the United States. The ASEAN + 3 (China, Japan, and South Korea) process is emerging as China's favorite vehicle in this regard, although the East Asia Summit, a larger convocation whose inaugural meeting was held in Malaysia in December 2005, is intended for a similar purpose.

China's strategic approach to Southeast Asia stands in stark contrast to the region's perception of U.S. engagement over the same period. While China seemed to be "walking the walk and talking the talk" of ASEAN, the United States appeared to view regional affairs entirely through the prism of the war on terrorism, while neglecting the region's other interests and challenges, such as economic development, environmental degradation, and infectious disease. Assertive U.S. foreign policy worldwide also went against the multilateral, confidence-building, consensual ethic of the region. U.S. impatience with regional "talk shops" and the "ASEAN way" has provided China a strategic opportunity to enhance its position in Southeast Asia, of which Beijing has clearly taken full advantage.

Russia

Although China and Russia have a history of deep mistrust that has not disappeared, this historical legacy is being mitigated today by an increasing array of common strategic interests and challenges. Russia has Chechnya; China has Taiwan and Xinjiang separatism. Russia bristles at NATO and Partnership for Peace nations extending around its periphery; China is likewise sensitive to the U.S. military presence and alliance partnerships on its doorstep. Moscow is suspicious of U.S. meddling in its internal affairs, charging that the United States, through non-governmental and governmental agents, has fomented "color revolutions" in former Soviet states to increase U.S. influence in the region and potentially induce similar changes in Russia; China has similar concerns.

As a result, China-Russia cooperation has intensified in a range of areas. Besides becoming an increasingly important supplier of Chinese energy, particularly oil, Russia remains China's largest supplier of defense platforms and technology. In August 2005, the two countries engaged in their first joint/combined military exercise, involving about 10,000 troops in an amphibious operation with echoes of a Taiwan scenario (although the exercise was framed as combating "terrorism, extremism, and separatism"[13]). While some observers viewed the exercise as a vehicle for Russia to sell China more weapons, questions remain about the future implications of growing military and other cooperation for the China-Russia strategic relationship, particularly given a converging commitment to constrain U.S. global power and influence.

IS MILITARY CONFLICT BETWEEN CHINA AND TAIWAN (AND THE UNITED STATES) INEVITABLE?

While the political situation across the Taiwan Strait remains far from resolution, military conflict between China and Taiwan is not inevitable. Were it to occur, however, it would very likely lead to serious political, and potentially military, conflict between the United States and China.

China's leaders have identified the goal of reunification with Taiwan as a "sacred duty of all Chinese people."[14] China's official policy on Taiwan calls for "peaceful reunification" under the "One Country, Two Systems" formula. In March 2005, the Chinese government passed the "Anti-Secession Law," codifying both China's peaceful unification policy and its intention to employ "non-peaceful means and other necessary measures" to prevent permanent separation.

The mainland views the current impasse as an internal matter left over from the Chinese civil war, when Chiang Kai-Shek's Republic of China government retreated to Taiwan and subsequently fell under the alliance protection of the United States. As discussed earlier, in the minds of China's leaders, the Taiwan issue is also inextricably linked to the legitimacy of Chinese Communist Party rule.

The Taiwan issue's hold on the Chinese people's imagination reflects the remarkable success of the Party's official propaganda over the past 50 years. A vast majority of the Chinese elite feels passionately that Taiwan is a part of China and that its eventual return to the "motherland" is essential to China's self-identity and honor. The success of Beijing's propaganda, however, is a double-edged sword for the leadership, arguably constraining its policy flexibility for fear of appearing weak on Taiwan.

China's tactics toward Taiwan are twofold. On the one hand, China seeks to cultivate closer economic, social, and cultural ties in a public effort to win over the Taiwan people's hearts and minds and promote peaceful reunification over time. In the process, Beijing has engaged in a classic "United Front" strategy: to extend benefits to those who are viewed as (relative) allies, while avoiding and seeking to isolate those with whom it disagrees. In practice, this has meant Beijing has reached out to the Kuomintang (KMT)/People's First Party (PFP) opposition, while refusing to deal with the elected Democratic Progressive Party (DPP) government.

Beijing demands that Taipei accept the "One China" principle as a precondition for re-opening talks. Taiwan President Chen Shui-bian calls for dialogue without preconditions, favors discussion of the meaning of "One China," and insists that the decision on Taiwan's future should be determined by the 23 million people in Taiwan. The absence of an authorized channel of communications between Taipei and Beijing has increased the chance of a conflict resulting from miscalculation or accident.

Meanwhile, the PRC continues to increase, upgrade, and modernize its military forces deployed opposite Taiwan, which Beijing claims is meant to deter independence. Others fear that China seeks to acquire the capability to coerce or take Taiwan by force sometime in the future. According to the U.S. Department of Defense, for instance, China has deployed and enhanced the accuracy of well over 700 mobile short-range ballistic missiles, which are being augmented by about 100 missiles each year.[15] Beijing has also deployed medium-range ballistic missiles, new land-attack cruise missiles, and other advanced naval and air capabilities across the Strait.

Indeed, China's military doctrine, force structure, defense acquisition strategy, planning, and operational training all appear focused primarily on a Taiwan scenario, including taking into account the possible intervention of the United States. These efforts, combined with political divisions in Taiwan that are constraining Taiwan's defense modernization, are shifting the military balance in the Taiwan Strait in Beijing's favor.

Burgeoning economic ties will likely have a stabilizing impact. Taiwan businesspeople have invested more than $100 billion in the mainland since the early 1990s, and two-way trade topped $80 billion in 2005.[16] But economic integration alone will not lead to amicable ties, much less to political integration. As generations pass, the connection of the Taiwan people to China, even of those whose mainland families escaped to the island in 1949, is becoming more tenuous, and a separate Taiwan national identity is developing in its stead. Nonetheless, maintaining the status quo remains the Taiwan population's overall preference.

The mainland's efforts to isolate Taiwan internationally, while increasingly successful, have done little to endear the mainland's leadership to the Taiwan people or government, or promote a sense that Beijing's "hearts and minds" campaign is anything more than a coercion campaign in disguise. Many observers believe that the only conditions under which Taiwan could accept unification would be upon the mainland's democratization, a prospect not immediately on the horizon.

In the past, China has identified several circumstances under which it would use force against Taiwan: a formal declaration of independence; an indefinite (*sine die*) delay in settlement of the issue; internal unrest on the island; foreign intervention in Taiwan's internal affairs, including establishment of a formal alliance or stationing of foreign forces; and acquisition of nuclear weapons. The Anti-Secession Law is more vague, claiming that any "act under any name or by any means to cause the fact of Taiwan's secession from China ... major incidents entailing Taiwan's secession from China ... or ... [should] possibilities for a peaceful reunification ... be completely exhausted" would serve as grounds for employment of "non-peaceful means and other necessary measures."[17]

The United States is implicated in the Taiwan issue due to its long-standing support for the island dating back to the Cold War, when Washington and Taipei had a formal treaty alliance. Following termination of the alliance, the United States has maintained its commitment to Taiwan's security under the Taiwan Relations Act (TRA), which authorizes Washington to provide Taiwan "with arms of a defensive character" to enable the island to maintain a "sufficient, self-defense capability."[18] According to the TRA, the United States would view "with grave concern" any Chinese attempt to coerce or attack Taiwan to achieve unification.

U.S. policy toward the Taiwan impasse has been primarily concerned with process; the United States has remained agnostic on the ultimate outcome of the dispute, but urges that any resolution be peaceful and non-coercive (thus pursuing a declared policy of "peaceful *resolution*" rather than Beijing's "peaceful *reunification*"). Washington has also declared its opposition to unilateral actions by either side to change the status quo.

China views U.S. involvement with Taiwan, particularly its arms sales and defense ties with the island, as an encouragement to Taiwan independence forces and a fundamental obstacle to unification. Nonetheless, as a result of Bush Administration actions to restrain President Chen Shui-bian, Beijing is more confident today than in the past that the United States will work to prevent Taiwan's drift toward independence in the near term.[19] Combined with China's increasing self-confidence about its growing political and economic power, and military capabilities, China seems to have concluded that time is on its side.

Rather than compel near-term unification, therefore, Beijing appears to be focusing on deterring independence, while postponing the task of reunification to the indefinite future. This approach is consistent with Beijing's focus on domestic development and securing a peaceful external environment. However, a change in the political landscape in Taiwan favoring independence, a perception that the United States is backing this position, or a domestic regime legitimacy crisis could lead to a heightened sense of urgency that tougher action, even military force, is necessary to prevent Taiwan's separation from the mainland. And should it become clear that Taipei has foreclosed the possibility of future unification, there is little doubt that Beijing would take military action, regardless of the potential political or economic price.

The United States will need to continue to exercise a policy of "dual deterrence" across the Taiwan Strait—encouraging decision makers in both Beijing and Taipei to remain patient, flexible, and constructive, and to avoid provocative actions that work against an eventual peaceful resolution of the impasse. Taipei will need to prevent good judgment from being overrun by domestic politics or frustration over its undefined international status. But ultimately, the ball is in China's court to display more creativity in its approach to Taiwan to truly win over the hearts and minds of the island's people in order to ensure the peaceful achievement of its "sacred" goal.

DOES CHINESE FOREIGN POLICY UPHOLD OR UNDERMINE THE INTERNATIONAL SYSTEM?

China has made a concerted effort to reassure the international community that its intentions are to uphold the basic tenets of the international system and to act consonant with international law. Beijing has affirmed the preeminent authority of international treaties and the United Nations as ultimate arbiters of international law and legitimacy for international actions. China often states its strong commitment to the "purpose and principles of the UN Charter," and has called on the UN to play a greater role in international affairs "as the core of the collective security mechanism."[20]

Since the late 1990s, China has recognized the political utility of multilateralism and internationalism to reassure others about the benign nature of China's rise and commitment to serving as a responsible international actor. Previously, China had been suspicious of multilateral structures that could potentially constrain Beijing's sovereignty and independent action, but its perspective changed as Beijing became reassured of its ability to safeguard its sovereign interests in multilateral environments, and it gradually came to appreciate the international system's benefits in addressing transnational challenges such as piracy, drug trafficking, terrorism, and infectious disease. China further recognized the value of being at the table to shape the rules, rather than having the rules imposed upon it. Today, China is a member of more than 130 inter-governmental international organizations, and has signed more than 250 international multilateral treaties.[21]

China's embrace of the United Nations is perhaps not surprising. Given China's generally defensive posture in international affairs, interest in reassuring the international community of its benign nature, and desire to mitigate U.S. power, Beijing's strategists recognize the practical utility of supporting UN principles that equalize the process, if not conduct, of international relations and constrain the ability of stronger powers to impose themselves on weaker states.

More critically, however, China is a permanent member of the UN Security Council, with veto power over all binding UN actions. This enables Beijing to safeguard its interests unconditionally within the UN system while technically remaining true to the principle of international law under UN authority. Although Beijing has rarely used its veto power, and then generally over Taiwan-related issues, this type of multilateralism is an ideal fit for China—allowing it to demonstrate its commitment to the international system, while preserving its power to prevent coercion or pressure from other nations.

Indeed, Beijing often defends its reluctance to impose sanctions or other penalties on offending regimes as a matter of principle—though, in practice, given China's own vulnerability on issues such as human rights, it is often as much about self-interest as concern for the international system. China's commitment to strict adherence to the principles of "state sovereignty" and "non-interference," for instance, has particular relevance to China given the Taiwan issue. China has been similarly reluctant to support humanitarian intervention and preemptive action for fear it may set a precedent that could be used to intervene in China.

"Non-interference" has also enabled China to defend its political and economic engagement with pariah nations, such as Zimbabwe, Sudan, and Burma, which, as discussed earlier, are sources of raw materials for China and whose brutal regimes have benefited greatly from China's largesse. In fact, Beijing has stated openly that its aid and investment in the developing world does not come with conditions. China's strong rhetorical support for international principles is somewhat relative, therefore, leading to actions that technically may conform to international law but which may compromise the international community's ability to protect international treaties, values, and norms around the world. While China may not be unique in this regard, its size and the lack of any domestic political constraints or checks on its international activities sets it apart from other nations.

On issues where its self-interest may conflict with international will, Beijing will often seek to prevent UN Security Council consideration, to avoid being put in the awkward position of voting one way or the other. Indeed, China has demonstrated great reluctance to be exposed or isolated as the primary obstacle to a generally accepted international action. In the UN Security Council, for instance, when Beijing recognizes it stands alone among permanent members in opposition to a resolution, China often abstains rather than vetoes. In this way, China can safeguard its good relations with the offending state while staying on the correct side of the international community by allowing the resolution to pass. An example was China's decision to abstain during the vote to authorize the first Iraq War in 1991, and in 2004 on the vote to condemn the atrocities in the Darfur region of Sudan (a resolution which itself had been watered down previously due to Chinese resistance). The day China stands alone to veto a UN Security Council resolution on an issue that does not affect it directly will signal a fundamental change in Chinese foreign policy and national self-confidence.

In the end, China appears little interested in altering the international system's rules of the game. However, the international community will have to determine whether the actions of a rising China result in weakening the system, regardless of China's intention.

IS CHINA'S RELATIONSHIP WITH JAPAN
DESTINED TO BE HOSTILE?

Given China's priority on maintaining a peaceful international environment and safeguarding key international economic relationships, China should have little interest in a hostile relationship with Japan. Sino-Japanese economic and trade relations have reached unprecedented levels, with bilateral trade reaching nearly $190 billion in 2005.[22] Japanese businesses served as China's third largest source of foreign investment that year, at more than $6 billion.[23] Japan has become China's second leading trade partner, behind the United States,[24] while China serves as Japan's leading trade partner.

However, relations in the political, military, and public arenas have significantly deteriorated in recent years as a mixture of heightened pride, self-confidence, and sense of historical grievance has fueled nationalism on both sides. Structural problems in the China-Japan relationship are increasing to a point where deeper and more lasting hostility between them is quite possible, with a real danger of confrontation in the absence of proactive and enlightened leadership from both sides.

Japanese textbooks that whitewash Japanese aggression in the 1930s and 1940s; Prime Minister Koizumi's annual visits to the Yasukuni Shrine, which commemorates Japan's warrior culture and enshrines 14 "Class A" war criminals from World War II; and the East China Sea territory/energy dispute[25] are sources of increased tension. Chinese resent what they perceive as lack of true remorse in Japan concerning its historical legacy, and fear that Tokyo's failure to account for its past at best shows disrespect for its victims, and at worst could permit future aggression. The Chinese Communist Party regime, meanwhile, has contributed to anti-Japan sentiment through its educational system and public propaganda over many years.

The problem goes much deeper, however. Never in history have China and Japan been strong powers at the same time. Given this unique circumstance, these two proud societies feel a natural sense of competition, and neither wants to be seen as succumbing to pressure from the other. This is especially true for China, which retains enormous bitterness over Japan's colonization of Taiwan and brutal occupation of China during the first half of the twentieth century.

China's public consciousness is such that even relatively minor offenses involving visiting Japanese students, businessmen, and China-Japan soccer matches lead to heated and sometimes violent reactions toward Japanese citizens and interests. Anti-Japan sentiment remains deeply instinctive in China, and is becoming a mark of patriotism.

China also views its relationship with Japan in the context of Tokyo's alliance with the United States. In the early 1970s, Mao Tse-tung urged President Nixon and Secretary of State Kissinger to take care of the alliance, calculating that it constrained Japan's remilitarization, and thus was not entirely against China's interest. Since the end of the Cold War, however, Beijing has grown increasingly concerned about the alliance's evolution in nature and purpose. The United States has encouraged Japan to cast off the pacifist constraints of the past 50 years (ironically imposed by a U.S.-drafted constitution) and be a more active security partner in regional and global affairs. China thus is revising its past judgment that the alliance serves as a "cork in the [Japanese] bottle" and growing increasingly worried about a more assertive alliance posture, for instance, in support of Taiwan.

Beijing protested vigorously when the United States and Japan publicly listed "peaceful resolution of issues concerning the Taiwan Strait through dialogue" as a common strategic objective for the alliance in February 2005.[26] Beijing also keeps a close eye on U.S. forces based in Okinawa and the Japanese mainland, Japan's interest in jointly developing ballistic missile defense with the United States, and Tokyo's overall commitment to modernizing its forces for their implications on a potential alliance "containment" strategy against China.

For its part, Japan is reacting to events on the mainland with increasing defiance and resentment over what it views as China's attempts to use history as a weapon to keep Japan humiliated and subjugated as China rises. Japanese popular opinion toward

China is at a historic low, fueled by a number of perceived provocations, such as the incursion of a Chinese nuclear submarine off the Okinawan coast in 2004, Beijing's opposition to Japan's bid for a permanent UN Security Council seat, China's own military build-up, and periodic anti-Japanese populist violence on the mainland. In December 2004, Japan took the extraordinary step of identifying China as a potential challenge to its security in its National Defense Program Outline, further reflecting Tokyo's evolving attitude toward Beijing and inflaming Chinese sentiment toward Japan.

Japan blames the Chinese government for fomenting anti-Japan sentiment to deflect the public's attention from its own deficiencies. In this way, Tokyo seems to absolve itself of any responsibility for creating, and thus taking steps to remedy, the increasingly hostile situation. Under such conditions, even many Japanese who oppose prime ministerial visits to the Yasukuni Shrine also oppose suspending such visits in response to pressure from China.

In this context, the East China Sea dispute epitomizes prevailing tensions and rising mutual suspicion. While the impasse is ostensibly about access to energy resources, the core issue is territory and sovereignty, with both sides seeking to safeguard their sovereign rights in an area of some strategic value. The situation remains a dangerous, increasingly militarized flashpoint, complicated and fueled by mutual mistrust and the lack of sustained senior-level dialogue. The impasse is thus vulnerable to miscalculation, accident, and escalation—and given the U.S. alliance with Japan, China-Japan conflict would pose a substantial challenge to U.S. foreign policy and U.S.-China relations, and jeopardize regional peace and stability.

China's leadership understands that the Japan issue is politically volatile. Beijing must give voice to Chinese pride and populist anger over perceived slights, but must also avoid fueling nationalist sentiment to the point where it loses control, or populist nationalism gets turned against the Beijing leadership itself. In the absence of Japanese concessions, however, particularly on prime ministerial visits to Yasukuni, Beijing will likely be unwilling and perhaps unable to prevent further deterioration in the relationship. The transition to Shinzo Abe as Japan's prime minister offers an opportunity for a fresh start in China-Japan relations.

In its language and tone, Beijing betrays confidence that over the course of coming decades, the balance in comprehensive national power between the two countries will shift in China's favor. Japanese sense this attitude, which adds to their sense of resentment and insecurity. China and Japan in fact have engaged in a potentially destructive action-reaction cycle fueled by deep populist antipathy and historical resentment toward one another. Adding U.S. (and Taiwan) elements to this mix will create fundamental challenges to maintaining a stable China-Japan bilateral relationship in years to come.

DO CHINESE AND U.S. INTERESTS CONVERGE ON THE KOREAN PENINSULA?

U.S. and Chinese interests converge on the Korean peninsula in several fundamental respects. Both seek a stable peninsula free of nuclear weapons; both support peaceful resolution of the North Korea nuclear problem through dialogue, and eventual North-South reunification; neither has much patience for North Korea's ideology, style, methods, closed society, or regime overall.

Nonetheless, U.S. and Chinese interests over Korea diverge in several key respects as well. Most fundamentally, while the United States places a premium on non-proliferation, China's interest in stability trumps its commitment to a nuclear weapons-free peninsula or regime change in North Korea. U.S. discussion about the need for regime change creates anxiety in Beijing over unrest along China's northeastern border. China also remains concerned that Korean reunification could bring American forces closer to its border; China tolerates U.S. military forces in South Korea, but hopes they will eventually be withdrawn. Finally, China, unlike the United States, pays little attention to North Korea's dismal human rights record.

While Beijing has touted the goal of Korean reunification, China tacitly has appreciated the peninsula's division in years past. North Korea, formerly China's only formal treaty partner, has historically served as a useful buffer against threats to China's northeastern periphery. China entered the Korean War in 1950 to prevent China from being vulnerable to U.S. forces racing up the peninsula. Beijing's continued interest in maintaining distance between itself and "foreign forces," and preventing foreign influence along its periphery, relates to its general desire to prevent encirclement and containment.

Despite these historic ties, China's relationship with North Korea has long been troubled. Even before their ideologies diverged in the late 1970s, China was frustrated by North Korea's apparent lack of appreciation for China's sacrifices on its behalf during the Korean War. Today, while China often faults the United States for its North Korea policy, Beijing bristles at Pyongyang's dangerous brinkmanship, which places Northeast Asia in the spotlight of Washington's security agenda and creates regional tension and pressures on U.S.-China relations.[27]

China continues to show frustration with the North's reluctance to reform itself. As the source of more than two-third's of the North's fuel and a third of the North's food,[28] Beijing has urged Pyongyang to follow China's economic reform and political control model, which it believes could maintain North Korea's viability over time while reducing the drain on Chinese resources. To this point, China has been generally unsuccessful in convincing North Korea to take its advice, although Kim Jong Il's visit to the highly developed Chinese cities of Shanghai and Guangzhou in January 2006 and other nascent economic reforms have offered Chinese leaders a ray of hope that North Korea may eventually institute Chinese-style economic reform.[29]

China's top priority is to ensure overall stability along its Korean periphery. The highest levels of popular protest in China exist in the border provinces adjacent to North Korea, where China hosts tens if not hundreds of thousands of Korean refugees, contributing to fears within the Chinese leadership that regime survival may be tied up in the area's stability. Beijing worries that turmoil in North Korea could spawn a massive influx of refugees across the border, overwhelming China's law-enforcement and humanitarian capabilities, and potentially fomenting unrest among the ethnic Korean population that would require PRC military action. For these reasons, and because China believes that managing the North Korean regime requires more inducement than pressure, Beijing is much warier than the United States of using direct action to pressure Pyongyang, whether military force, sanctions, isolation strategies (including the Proliferation Security Initiative), or other such policies.

China's perspective toward stability and security on its periphery has likewise informed Beijing's handling of the North Korean nuclear weapons issue. China has consistently demanded that the North Korean nuclear impasse be solved peacefully through dialogue. Beijing has gone so far as to assume the role of host and broker during the Six Party talks in an effort to find common ground between the United States and North Korea that will promote progress toward a final agreement. While China has avoided taking sides in the dispute, the Chinese insist that North Korea is serious in its vow to give up its nuclear weapons program in return for security assurances, economic assistance, and a promise from Washington to work toward diplomatic recognition.

Nonetheless, while frustrated by the North's nuclear weapons policy and desirous of a resolution that leads to a non-nuclear peninsula, Beijing will likely be content with the status quo impasse as long as stability on the peninsula is maintained. Indeed, Beijing seems to be committed to a policy of dialogue at all costs. This policy reflects, in part, its worry that should dialogue fail, it will be obliged to put muscle behind its official mantra to "not tolerate" a nuclear North Korea—something it is loath to do, as indicated above.

Some in the United States complain that China could do more diplomatically and otherwise to bring North Korea to heel. While it is true China could do more, it is unlikely that Beijing has the influence to force Pyongyang against its wishes to give up its one diplomatic and military trump card, even if Beijing considered it in its interest to take more assertive action. Chinese officials also note that were they to sanction North Korea, they would lose any ability to exercise influence on Pyongyang and drive the regime into a corner, which they claim would prove dangerous and counterproductive.

North Korea's missile and nuclear weapons tests in 2006, conducted over China's strong opposition, enraged China and placed it in an awkward position. Beijing remains worried that such a clear demonstration of North Korea's nuclear weapons capability could eventually lead Japan—and perhaps Taiwan—to reconsider its non-nuclear posture. China supported UN Security Council resolutions condemning the tests, including one after the nuclear test that mandated international sanctions. Nonetheless, China remains strongly committed to a diplomatic approach to solve the impasse and generally opposed to isolation or pressure strategies against the North, although debates about possible changes in its North Korea policy continue within Chinese leadership and academic circles.

South Korea shares China's paramount interest in stability on the peninsula. The China-South Korea relationship has warmed markedly in recent years, leading to questions about whether Beijing is taking advantage of recent tensions in South Korea's relations with the United States to drive a wedge in the US-ROK alliance. China has become South Korea's largest export market and trade partner,[30] and a critical element of Seoul's economic recovery since the late 1990s. While there are indications that Seoul is becoming uncomfortable with growing Chinese influence in North Korea, South Korea's President Roh Moo-hyun nonetheless has spoken in recent years about pursuing an "independent foreign policy," and serving as a "balancer" in regional affairs, language that plays well in China and rather poorly in the United States. South Korea has been particularly reluctant to accept the notion that U.S. forces stationed on the peninsula may be used elsewhere, including in a Taiwan military contingency, which also pleases the mainland.

Seoul will likely accommodate more readily than Tokyo to China's rise. Nonetheless, South Korea, like others in the region, is nervous about the full implications of a rising China, and in the end will likely want to maintain its alliance with the United

States as a strategic hedge, particularly if Seoul is not forced to support a hostile U.S. posture toward China (and North Korea). Beijing meanwhile clearly wants South Korea to align itself more closely with China, but takes a subtle approach—consistent with its desire not to push Seoul too quickly or antagonize the United States in the process.

WHY IS CHINA STRENGTHENING ITS MILITARY?

China's defense establishment remains highly opaque, which complicates objective and fully confident outside assessments about its intentions, capabilities, and resources dedicated to national defense.[31] Nonetheless, China's 2004 Defense White Paper made clear Beijing's emphasis on the "increasing importance of the military element of national power."[32] The 1991 Gulf War and 1995–6 Taiwan Strait crisis were wake-up calls to the Chinese leadership and the People's Liberation Army (PLA) concerning their ability to handle a Taiwan scenario, including potential U.S. intervention. Then, in 1999, assessments about political trends in both Taiwan and the United States led Beijing to renew and accelerate its emphasis on comprehensively developing and recalibrating China's military in doctrine, training, education, force structure, and overall operational capability.

China has justified its military modernization as the reasonable action of a major power seeking to update antiquated weapons systems and equipment, and rationalize an outdated military structure. Beijing policy makers note China's history of vulnerability to external aggression and express commitment to a defensive posture to ensure the protection of national sovereignty and territorial integrity. In practice, defense of sovereignty and territorial integrity has translated in large part into preparations for a Taiwan scenario. Chinese leaders say its military development serves as a "deterrent" against Taiwan independence; others fear that China is developing a decisive operational capability to take Taiwan by force.

China's Military Spending

China's 2006 defense budget of $35.1 billion is an increase of 14.7 percent over 2005,[33] which itself was double China's defense budget in 2000. These figures, however, are open to significant debate given the lack of transparency in China's military establishment and China's tendency to under-report its defense spending (see Table 5.2). Outside estimates of China's actual annual defense outlays are based on a number of items not included in China's official military budget, including expenditures on foreign arms procurement, expenses related to the People's Armed Police, funding for nuclear weapons stockpiles and the Second Artillery, earnings from military commercial ventures and foreign arms sales, defense industry and conversion subsidies, defense-related research and development, and operations and maintenance costs shared with local, provincial, or regional governments. Assuming China's defense expenditure as a proportion of GDP remains constant, China's defense spending, according to a modest estimate, could rise more than threefold, to $185 billion, by 2025.

TABLE 5.2 Competing Statistics on China's Military Expenditure, 2005 (billions of $)

	Official budget[i]	SIPRI[ii]	RAND[iii]	CFR[iv]	DoD[v]
Absolute expenditure (US$)	29.9	35.4	42–51	44–67	60–90

[i] *Source:* Office of the Secretary of Defense, Annual Report to Congress: *The Military Power of the People's Republic of China 2005* (Washington, D.C.: United States Department of Defense, 2005), 21.

[ii] *Source:* SIPRI (Stockholm International Peace Research Institute), *SIPRI Yearbook 2005: Armaments, Disarmament and International Security* (Oxford: Oxford University Press, 2005), 318.

[iii] This calculation is based on RAND's estimate that actual defense spending is 1.4–1.7 times China's official figure. *Source:* RAND Corporation Project Air Force, *Modernizing China's Military: Opportunities and Constraints* (RAND, 2005), 134.

[iv] 2003 figure: *Source:* Council on Foreign Relations, *Independent Taskforce on Chinese Military Power*, 2003, 5.

[v] *Source:* Office of the Secretary of Defense, Annual Report to Congress: *The Military Power of the People's Republic of China 2005* (Washington, D.C.: United States Department of Defense, 2005), 22.

China has closely observed and assessed U.S. military operations since the first Gulf War, using lessons learned to drive its own military modernization. China's 2004 White Paper, for instance, introduced a new doctrinal concept of preparing to fight "local wars under conditions of informationalization"[34]—a change in terminology from the 1990s-era concept of "local wars under modern high-tech conditions," which demonstrates Beijing's recognition of information technology's growing importance in modern warfare, as reflected in U.S. military operations over the past decade.

China's doctrinal concept of "active defense" is the doctrine of the weak against the strong. Although defensive in purpose, the doctrine seeks to take the initiative and stay on the offensive from a conflict's earliest stages in order to bring hostilities to a swift conclusion. This concept is matched with a doctrine that puts a premium on surprise, preemption, indirect/asymmetrical confrontation, and concentrated strikes on an opponent's most critical platforms and capabilities, particularly its C4ISR (command, control, communications, computer, information, surveillance, and reconnaissance) systems, and on high-value psychological targets in an effort to overwhelm and undermine an opponent's will to resist in the early stages of conflict. Likewise, China is focusing intently on anti-access, area-denial strategies, procuring platforms with the capability and intention to deter, prevent, or complicate the intervention of the United States (or others) in a Taiwan scenario.

With regard to its strategic nuclear weapons, China adheres to a "no first use" doctrine and "minimum deterrent" posture, in which Beijing deploys just enough nuclear weapons to feel confident about retaining a survivable, second-strike counter-value capability. In recent years, some experts have questioned whether China will alter these long-standing doctrines. As yet there is no indication of change, although some in the PLA have advocated amending the "no first use" doctrine due to concerns about potential precision strikes on its nuclear facilities, or other unconventional weapon attacks.

In implementing its new doctrinal and strategic concepts, Beijing has streamlined the military to create a more professional, efficient fighting force. In 2005, the PLA cut its forces by 200,000 to 2.3 million active-duty personnel.[35] At the same time, Beijing has augmented military training, recruited more educated personnel, and is engaging in more comprehensive and realistic military exercises. The PLA has focused in particular on developing greater "joint" capability among the military services to increase effectiveness and efficiency, although the effort has met with limited success.

China's security focus has shifted from continental concerns to its maritime periphery, leading to a growing emphasis on China's air and naval capabilities. This is reflected in China's resource allocation, procurement strategy, and structural changes in its defense establishment, with ground forces being thinned to a historic low and downgraded relative to the other services. The Second Artillery missile force is also receiving an increasing share of resources, with particular attention to China's rapidly increasing SRBM (short-range ballistic missile) deployments opposite Taiwan. The PLA is upgrading its longer-range missiles on land and (under)sea by extending their reach, shifting from liquid- to solid-fuel, and improving precision guidance. China's long-range missiles are expected to be able to reach the entire continental United States as early as 2010.

Defense industry reforms that began in the late 1990s have helped improve China's indigenous military industry, particularly in aerospace/missiles, shipbuilding, and information technology. Nonetheless, Beijing continues to rely on foreign suppliers for most advanced platforms and technologies. Russia continues to be China's primary source for advanced items, which in recent years have included, *inter alia*, quiet and capable diesel submarines with advanced long-range anti-ship cruise missiles; advanced destroyers outfitted with anti-carrier missiles; third and fourth generation fighter aircraft capable of long-range, precision strike operations; AWACS and tanker aircraft; and short-range missiles. Each of these platforms has direct relevance to a Taiwan scenario, including potential U.S. intervention.

Due to the potential impact of Chinese military modernization on U.S. military commitments and operations in East Asia, the United States maintains an arms embargo on China imposed after the 1989 Tiananmen Square incident, and has pressured the EU not to lift its similar embargo. In recent years, Washington has also leaned hard on Israel to curb its defense assistance to China.

Beijing outsources certain military assignments to civilian industry, promotes acquisition of dual-use technologies, and often integrates civilian and military production. Beijing's domestic industry is attempting to develop anti-satellite weapons to challenge U.S. information dominance. China's shipbuilding industry services both civilian and military vessels, while the PLA has taken the lead in laying China's national fiber optic telecommunications network. China's space program, which in 2003 put its first man into orbit, is also closely connected with China's military, and is one arena in which China has shown advanced indigenous capability.

In concert with reform and modernization of PLA doctrine, organization, and equipment, China's military leaders are also looking to modernize and streamline the logistics and mobilization systems that support military operations. Over the past decade, Beijing has strengthened civil-military integration through an enhanced national defense mobilization system designed to enable the PLA to draw from civilian resources—such as transportation, communications, air defense, internal security (police), and commodity supply networks—to support military operations in a crisis. These efforts have also included a revitalization of the reserve and militia system in China, and experimental reforms of the PLA's logistics infrastructure.

While China's increasing commitment to military modernization over the last several years has led to progress in PLA capabilities, it has also highlighted a number of glaring deficiencies and vulnerabilities. These include limited joint (multi-service) operations capability and support systems, a nascent NCO (non-commissioned officer) corps, poorly educated personnel for high-tech warfare assignments, increasing dependence on imported energy resources, shortage of spare parts and maintenance for increasingly sophisticated weapons systems, and limited operational experience. China is currently not able to engage in effective power projection. Its procurement or development of aircraft carriers, heavy bombers, long-range amphibious ships, military transport aircraft, and global surveillance and communications satellites would signal a change of Chinese doctrine and intentions in this regard, although their operational integration into an effective fighting force would remain a key challenge.

Beijing seems to understand its limitations at present. Chinese leaders have no illusions that the PLA is a match for the U.S. military, will catch up in the foreseeable future, or will measurably narrow the gap in comprehensive national power for decades, at least. What China does seek is to focus on niche capabilities and U.S. vulnerabilities to deter, complicate, and delay, if not defeat, U.S. intervention in a Taiwan scenario, while more broadly preventing the United States and its allies from violating its sovereignty or containing China's development through military action or intimidation.

While a Taiwan scenario may serve as a leading motivating factor for China's military modernization efforts, operational capabilities developed in the process need not be confined to Taiwan but may have broader applications to assert Chinese interests beyond the Taiwan Strait. Regardless of China's primary focus on Taiwan and the United States, its military development will have impact on the overall regional balance of power that will require, at least, greater transparency to provide sufficient reassurance to other states concerned about the rising giant on their shores.

6

Conclusion: Toward a New
United States–China Relationship

The rise of China, especially in economic terms but also as a major player in global security and political affairs, is one of the most momentous developments of our time. It parallels, in many respects, the rise of the United States itself in the late nineteenth century and will almost certainly supersede in importance the rise of Japan in the second half of the twentieth century. This emergence of China to global salience, as well as the many unique features of its advent, pose new and unprecedented challenges for the United States, the world's only present superpower, and the global community in both economic and military terms.

Four fundamental conclusions for U.S. policy emerge from our assessment of China's current position and future prospects. First, China clearly represents both an opportunity *and* threat to the United States in economic and security terms. Second, the extent to which China becomes either an opportunity or a challenge is not predetermined but will depend greatly on the policy choices and internal dynamics of China and the United States in coming years. Third, while U.S. influence over China should not be overstated, U.S. policy can play a role, for good or ill, in shaping the decisions China makes about its future. Finally, therefore, while a responsible strategic approach toward China must include preparation of U.S. domestic, foreign, and defense policies to deter and deflect Chinese actions that are contrary to U.S. interests, the United States has an overriding stake in pursuing a strategy that effectively integrates China into the global economic and security systems in a way that reinforces the American people's long-term security, prosperity, and peace.

The timing is right, and the logic overwhelming, for both countries to pursue a constructive relationship. For the foreseeable future, Beijing will be consumed with a series of difficult domestic transitions that will require a peaceful international environment and good relations with the United States in particular. The United States, for its part, is preoccupied with threats from *jihadist* extremism, rogue regimes, failed or failing states, and weapons proliferation—challenges Washington needs substantial international cooperation to meet, including cooperation from China.

Even more compelling is the fact that in spite of a number of important differences, China and the United States share a large and growing number of common security and economic interests. Adroit management of these issues, and of the bilateral relationship itself, can exploit this convergence to maximize the opportunities for cooperation and minimize the risks of confrontation.

On the security front, as nuclear powers, China and the United States have a strong common interest in avoiding proliferation of weapons to non-nuclear states. This interest is particularly keen in the East Asia region, where the two countries have fought extensive wars (both with and against each other) over the past century. Both the United States and China have powerful national interests in countering terrorism around the world, and in working together to prevent the emergence of failed states that could become breeding grounds for terrorist activity and regional instability. They have a particular joint interest in avoiding hostilities in the Taiwan Strait, which could derail China's priority strategy of economic development as well as embroil the region in conflict.

On the economic side, the two deeply globalized countries also have substantial common interests. Both would suffer severely from global economic and financial instability, as could readily occur from a precipitous fall of the dollar and/or a renewed sharp rise in oil prices. Both would lose from the seizing up of the world trading system that could evolve from an outbreak of protectionism in the U.S. Congress. Both therefore have a major stake in reducing the present trade and current account imbalances to a sustainable level. The United States and China in fact have powerful incentives to find ways to cooperate effectively, both bilaterally and with the world's other key economies, to steer global economic and financial developments in constructive directions. Success in such efforts would also likely reduce the instances of serious friction between the two countries themselves and enhance the prospects for resolving such frictions harmoniously when they do appear.

The two countries also share common interests regarding China's domestic development. Neither wishes to see an unstable, collapsing, or anarchic China, and both recognize the benefits of that country's continued prosperity and stability. Both understand the benefits of domestic reform in China and the need to move toward a social and political system that is both more responsive to the needs of its citizens and will support a pattern of future economic growth more consistent with international equilibrium. The United States and China also share an interest in avoiding the downsides of China's current economic modernization, which may contribute to both Chinese domestic and broader transnational challenges, such as pollution, emergent infectious diseases, organized crime, and trafficking in weapons, drugs, and people.

China and the United States have similar interests on a range of issues that straddle economics, security, and China's domestic development, even when their current behavior may suggest the opposite. As the world's two largest energy consumers, the United States and China have major common interests both in generating further improvements in their own energy efficiencies and in mitigating global supply shortages. Rather than scrambling for "preferred access" deals, which are chimerical in any event because of the global nature of the oil market, the United States and China should be on the same side of the table in virtually all international energy discussions, including at the International Energy Agency. Similarly, as the world's two largest emitters of greenhouse gases, the United States and China should be on the same page with regard to reducing pollution and mitigating global warming and climate change. Stemming the global spread of infectious diseases—such as HIV/AIDS and avian influenza—is another pressing area of common concern.

Yet shared security interests, economic integration, and common cross-border concerns are not necessarily enough to prevent clashing priorities, official miscalculation, mistrust, or populist emotions in either country from plunging the relationship into conflict, if not crisis, in coming years. On economic and trade issues, the two countries have different views on the need for China to revalue its currency substantially and to take tougher measures to crack down on violations of intellectual property rights. They also differ frequently on their respective security and diplomatic roles in East and Central Asia. The Taiwan question remains unresolved, with many in the United States increasingly concerned about the implications of China's continued military development for the potential use of force to unify Taiwan with the mainland. Washington is likewise suspicious about China's strategic intentions toward future U.S. involvement and influence in East Asian affairs. Beijing's good relations with such regimes as Iran, Burma, and Sudan are often at odds with U.S. interests. The American people will also continue to have serious problems with much of China's political situation, especially ongoing human rights abuses; restrictions on the press, internet, and religious practices; and violent crackdowns on social unrest.

Both countries will require significant shifts in their present mindsets to realize their common interests and indeed to reduce the risk of confrontational scenarios in the future. To begin, they will need to redouble current efforts to resolve bilateral problems, while at the same time steadily working to alleviate strategic mistrust that lingers beneath the surface of the relationship.

Assuming China's continued rise, the United States will need to engage China as a full economic and political partner on the global stage, at least in parallel with its traditional partners from the European Union and Japan, while also taking Chinese strategic interests more seriously into account. Washington also will need to be prepared psychologically for the impact China's rise may have on the relative power and influence of the United States in East Asia and beyond. While China is unlikely to challenge this preeminence in political, economic, or military power for the foreseeable future, the rise in China's relative power will likely lead to, or at least be associated with, economic dislocations in the United States, and may alter U.S. strategic relationships with friends and even allies around the world as nations accommodate themselves to China's new status.

Even in the face of a failing or chaotic China, the interests of the United States and its global partners would be best served by policies that seek to engage rather than isolate the country, in order to moderate the potentially devastating economic and security outcomes of such a scenario.

For its part, China will have to take on the global responsibilities commensurate with its size and influence. Beijing can no longer claim that a foreign policy premised on a desperate need for internal development is a purely domestic matter, particularly when it facilitates the violation of international norms by unsavory regimes. Nor can Beijing fall back on a "developing world" self-image to deny its own impact on international affairs: The policies and actions of a rapidly developing and globally integrated nation of 1.3 billion people necessarily will affect the management of a peaceful and stable global system. As China rises, Beijing will need to acknowledge this fact and start acting in ways that reinforce international norms and that reflect a broader and more long-term concept of China's self-interest—becoming what U.S. Deputy Secretary of State Robert Zoellick calls a "responsible stakeholder."

Beijing will also need to accept and sustain long-standing American interests in the stability and prosperity of Asia, including the critical security and economic role of such partners as

Japan, while maintaining its stated preference to resolve its dispute with Taiwan peacefully. Finally, China will need to steadily reform its social and political system, including through the development of transparent and accountable institutions, to meet the needs of its citizens, avoid widespread social unrest, and realize the kind of sociopolitical achievements seen in other current and emergent major powers such as the United States, Europe, Japan, India, and Brazil.

It will obviously take a good deal of time and intellectual energy to bring such a strategic framework to full fruition, and there will be inevitable disagreements and setbacks along the way. Fortunately, however, the process has already begun via the Senior Dialogue launched in 2005 by Deputy Secretary Zoellick and his counterparts at the Ministry of Foreign Affairs and the National Development and Reform Commission in Beijing. The group met twice during its first year of operation and aims to provide an overarching context within which to consider the whole range of issues that confront the two countries in their relationship, especially those that cut across the usual economic and security contexts and thus are particularly difficult to address. The early results of the effort appear promising, if still at a very preliminary stage, reinforcing the view that the United States and China can and should work candidly and constructively together to resolve bilateral differences and address global problems of mutual concern.

We strongly believe that the overriding issues at this point in time are (1) how the two countries think about each other and (2) the initiation of a process that will eventually provide a mutually beneficial, and hence sustainable, framework within which they can conduct their relationship for the years and perhaps decades ahead. This volume has attempted to take the first step in formulating sound policy through such a process: to set forth a factual and analytic framework that captures the essentials of China today across the four critical domains of its domestic economy, its domestic sociopolitical interests, its role in the world economy, and its posture on national security and foreign policy.

The United States and China will soon be, if they are not already, the two most important countries in the world. Sober-minded management of their critical and evolving relationship in the coming decades will be the ultimate challenge for both, with serious implications not only for their two countries, but the stability and well-being of the global community as a whole.

Our balance sheet suggests that the areas of mutual interest between the United States and China are more prevalent, and more significant, than their spheres of potential conflict. That should be encouraging to both countries and both peoples. We acknowledge, however, that many U.S. and Chinese observers alike are more pessimistic in their views, and that the United States and China have serious bilateral problems that must be addressed and resolved before the relationship can reach its true potential.

For all these reasons, we believe an informed, sustained, open debate is essential in both countries—both to better evaluate present realities, and to enable a future relationship that is mutually beneficial. This volume has been our initial attempt to provide a comprehensive guide and resource to that end.

Notes

CHINA'S DOMESTIC ECONOMY: CONTINUED GROWTH OR COLLAPSE?

1. In December 2005, the National Bureau of Statistics issued a revised 2004 GDP level number 16.8 percent higher than that previously announced. In January 2006, it issued a revised GDP series for the years 1993–2003. The revised GDP data, which largely reflect previously unmeasured services output, are measured from the production side. The Statistical Bureau also is expected to provide data on GDP disaggregated into investment, consumption, and so forth. When possible, this chapter's analysis is based on the revised production side GDP data; some of the analysis is based on anticipated revised GDP expenditure data.

2. Measured in terms of purchasing power parity (PPP), which is an attempt to take into account the effect of different price levels prevailing in different countries, the World Bank has ranked China as the world's second largest economy since 1995. For reasons explained below, we do not believe that World Bank estimates of China's GDP measured in terms of PPP should be taken seriously.

3. By the World Bank's two absolute poverty standards of $1 and $2 per day, the number of Chinese still living below the poverty line is many times larger than 26 million. But the proportionate reduction in the number living below these poverty lines also is very large.

4. Extrapolations from 2004 gross domestic product are at the average annual growth rates for 1993–2004, 9.6 percent for China and 3.3 percent for the United States.

5. United Nations Population Division, "World Population Prospects: The 2004 Revision Population Data Base," 2005, http://esa.un.org/unp/p2k0data.asp, accessed January 9, 2006.

6. The trade share of GDP is the ratio of imports plus exports to GDP.

7. Organization for Economic Cooperation and Development, *China* (Paris: OECD, 2005), 32.

8. World Bank, *World Development Report 1982* (Washington: World Bank, 1982), 154.

9. World Bank, *World Development Report 1996* (Washington: World Bank, 1996), 200.

10. OECD, *China*, 32–33. International Monetary Fund, "People's Republic of China: 2005 Article IV Consultation, November 2005, 12, www.i.org/external/pubs/ft/scr/2005/cr05411.pdf, accessed November 18, 2005.

11. Martin Wolf, "Why is China Growing So Slowly?" *Foreign Policy* (January-February 2005), http://www.foreignpolicy.com/sty/cms.php?story_id=2750&ge=1, accessed August 4, 2005.

12. The transaction includes an option for Bank of America to increase its ownership stake to 19.9 percent at any time prior to March 1, 2011.

13. People's Bank of China, "China Monetary Policy Report, Quarter Two, 2005," August 8, 2005, 28–29, www.pbc.gov.cn, accessed August 10, 2005.

14. Louis Kuijs, "Investment and Saving in China," World Bank Research Paper No. 1, May 2005, 8.

15. In 2002, China introduced a Rural Cooperative Medical Scheme to provide partial medical insurance to rural households. Its coverage remains quite limited but the state hopes to expand it to cover as much as 40 to 60 percent of the rural population by year-end 2007.

16. Excludes capital expenditures.

17. For more on the social reasons for expanding these programs, see the analysis in the section "Social Policy Issues" in this chapter as well as the discussion in Chapter 3.

18. Azizur Rahman Kahn and Carl Riskin, "China's Household Income and Its Distribution, 1995 and 2002," *China Quarterly*, 182 (June 2005): 358.

19. Sang Ke, "Major investment urged in urban water supply market," *China Economic News*, July 11, 2005, 3.

20. Jian Dong, "China stresses imminence of changing extensive economic development model," *China Economic News*, August 1, 2005, 1–2.

21. International Energy Agency, "Oil Market Report," May 12, 2004 and July 13, 2005, www.oilmarketreport.org, accessed May 15, 2004 and August 5, 2005, respectively.

22. Jonathan Anderson, *How to Think About China (Part 5): The Main Drivers of Medium Term Growth*, UBS Investment Research, Asian Economic Perspectives, November 14, 2005, 27, 43.

23. State Council, "Notice concerning key points in the carrying out well the work of building a resource saving society," July 6, 2005, http://www.china.org.cn/chinese/PI-c/907695.htm, accessed August 3, 2005.

24. National Development and Reform Commission, "China Medium and Long Term Energy Conservation Plan," November 24, 2004, http://www.beconchina.or/energy_saving.htm, accessed August 3, 2005.

25. "The Proposals of the CPC Central Committee on Drafting the 11th Five-Year Plan," approved October 11, 2005, http://www.sdpc.gov.cn/printpage.htm, accessed October 19, 2005.

26. World Bank Office, Beijing, "Quarterly Update," February 2006, 15, http://siteresources.worldbank.org/INTCHINA/Resources/318862-1121421293578/cqu_feb06.pdf, accessed January 21, 2006.

27. National Bureau of Statistics of China, *China Statistical Yearbook 2005* (Beijing: Statistical Publishing House, 2005), 255 and the revised GDP numbers issued January 2006, www.stats.gov.cn, accessed January 9, 2006.

28. Liu Manping, "Oil pricing reforms must be pursued with caution," *China Daily*, Sept. 20, 2006, 4.

29. Nicholas R. Lardy, *Integrating China into the Global Economy* (Washington D.C.: Brookings Institution Press, 2002), 75–79, 91–94.

30. Daniel H. Rosen, Scott Rozelle, and Jikun Huang, *Roots of Competitiveness: China's Evolving Agriculture Interests* (Washington D.C.: Peterson Institute for International Economics, July 2004).

31. National Bureau of Statistics, *China Statistical Yearbook 2005* (Beijing: China Statistics Press, 2005), 359; *China Statistical Abstract 2005* (Beijing: China Statistics Press, 2005), 104.

32. National Bureau of Statistics, *China Statistical Abstract 2005*, 18, 67.

33. Nicholas R. Lardy, "State-Owned Banks in China," in *The Future of State-Owned Financial Institutions*, ed. Gerard Caprio et al. (Washington D.C.: Brookings Institution Press, 2004), 112.

CHINA'S DOMESTIC TRANSFORMATION: DEMOCRATIZATION OR DISORDER?

1. Data drawn from Murray Scot Tanner, "China Rethinks Unrest," *Washington Quarterly* (Summer 2004) and "Chinese Government Responses to Rising Social Unrest," testimony for the U.S.-China Economic and Security Review Commission hearing *China's State Control Mechanisms and Methods*, April 14, 2005, http://www.uscc.gov/hearings/2005hearings/written_testimonies/05_04_14wrts/tanner_murray_wrts.htm, accessed March 2, 2006. See also Mainland Affairs Council, "Jinqi Zhongguo Dalu Shehui Quntixing Kangzheng Shijian Fenxi" ["An Analysis on the Recent Trend of Mass Group Incidents in China"], http://www.mac.gov.tw/big5/cnews/ref940829.htm, accessed December 19, 2005; "PRC Public Security Ministry Spokesman Says Public Order Disturbances Up 6.6 percent," *Xinhua*, January 19, 2006; Francesco Sisci, "Is China Headed for a Social 'Red Alert'?," *Asia Times*, October 20, 2005.

2. "Significant Shift in Focus of Peasants' Rights Activism: An Interview with Rural Development Researcher Yu Jianrong of the Chinese Academy of Social Sciences," http://www.chinaelections.org/en/readnews.asp?newsid=%7BA0B4FFF9-1F57-460D-BBB3824B59420C2F%7D, accessed December 19, 2005.

3. "Text of Communique Issued by Fifth Plenum of 16th CPC Central Committee," *Xinhua*, October 11, 2005, in Open Source Center, CPP20051011062054.

4. "'People Power' Aids Green Drive in China," *Straits Times*, November 15, 2005.

5. *Transparency International Corruption Perceptions Index 2005*, http://www.transparency.org/policy_and_research/surveys_indices/cpi/2005, accessed January 23, 2006.

6. Lu Xiaobo, "Corruption and Regime Legitimacy in China," in *China's New Politics*, ed. Francois Godement (Paris: La Documentation Français, 2003).

7. Organization for Economic Cooperation and Development, *Governance in China: Fighting Corruption in China* (Paris: OECD, 2005), http://miranda.sourceoecd.org/vl=4368929/cl=11/nw=1/rpsv/~6677/v2005n25/s6/p129, accessed January 30, 2006.

8. "Labor Shortage Emerges in Guangdong," *Xinhua*, August 9, 2004.

9. Richard Jackson and Neil Howe, *The Graying of the Middle Kingdom: The Demographics and Economics of Retirement Policy in China* (Washington, D.C: Center for Strategic and International Studies, 2004), 3.

10. Data from National Population and Family Planning Commission, http://www.npfpc.gov.cn, accessed January 10, 2006.

11. "Warning over China's Aging Populace," *China Daily*, June 12, 2004.

12. United Nations Population Fund, *Sex Ratio-Facts and Figures*, July 2004, http://www.unfpa.org/swp/2005/english/boxsources.htm #source1, accessed January 12, 2006.

13. Valerie Hudson and Andrea den Boer, *Bare Branches: The Security Implications of Asia's Surplus Male Population* (Cambridge, Mass: The MIT Press, 2004), 186.

14. *Education in China: Lessons for U.S. Educators* (New York: Asia Society, 2005).

15. National Bureau of Statistics of China, *China Statistical Yearbook 2004: Basic Statistics on Education*, http://www.stats.gov.cn, accessed December 11, 2005.

16. National Bureau of Statistics and Ministry of Finance, *Communique on 2004 Education Spending by the Ministry of Education*, http://www.moe.edu.cn/edoas/website18/info17959.htm, accessed December 22, 2005.

17. Regulations issued in January 2006, stipulate that miscellaneous fees must be abolished and subsidies for education expenses made available to impoverished rural families by 2008. "Wen Jiabao Airs Views on Rural Issues," *Xinhua*, January 29, 2006.

18. Ministry of Education, *2004 Announcement on Education*

Development Statistics, April 2005, http://www.moe.edu.cn/edoas/website18/info17959.htm, accessed December 22, 2005.

19. United Nations Development Program *Human Development Report 2005,* http://hdr.undp.org/reports/global/2005/pdf/HDR05_HDI.pdf, accessed January 23, 2006.

20. "The Medical Reform Controversy," *Beijing Review,* vol. 48, no. 38 (September 2005).

21. Bates Gill, J. Stephen Morrison, and Andrew Thompson, *Defusing China's Time Bomb: Sustaining the Momentum of China's HIV/AIDS Response* (Washington, D.C.: Center for Strategic and International Studies, June 2004).

22. *2005 Update on the HIV/AIDS Epidemic and Response in China* (Beijing: Chinese Center for Disease Control and Prevention, January 24, 2006).

23. World Health Organization, "Avian influenza—situation in China—update 2," January 25, 2006, www.who.int, accessed February 20, 2006.

24. World Health Organization, *The Impact of Chronic Disease in China, 2005,* www.who.int/chp/chronic_disease-report/en, accessed January 18, 2006.

25. *Human Development Report 2005* (New York: United Nations Development Programme, 2005), 241, http://hdr.undp.org/reports/global/2005/pdf/HDR05_HDI.pdf, accessed January 14, 2006.

26. Jackson and Howe, *Graying of the Middle Kingdom.*

27. "The Chinese Miracle Will End Soon," *Der Speigel,* March 7, 2005, http://hdr.undp.org/reports/global/2005/pdf/HDR05_HDI.pdf, accessed January 14, 2006.

28. Christopher Flavin and Gary Gardner, *China, India, and the New World Order: State of the World 2006* (Washington, D.C.: Worldwatch Institute, 2006), 3–23.

29. "Seeds of a Clean, Green City," *South China Morning Post,* September 1, 2004.

30. Ma Jun interview, *Marketplace,* American Public Media, January 20, 2006, http://marketplace.publicradio.org/features/china2006, accessed January 20, 2006.

31. "CPC Document Says Enhancing Party's Ability To Govern 'Major Strategic Subject,'" *Xinhua,* September 26, 2004.

32. "80 percent of Farmers Vote in Village Committee Elections," *China Daily*, September 7, 2005.

33. Joseph Fewsmith, "Taizhou Area Explores Ways to Improve Local Governance," *China Leadership Monitor*, no. 15 (Summer 2005).

34. Minxin Pei, "Creeping Democratization in China," *Journal of Democracy*, vol. 6, no. 4 (October 1995), 73.

35. General Office of Chinese Communist Party Central Committee and State Council, *Circular Concerning Improving Village Committee Election*, reference no. 2002–14, 2002.

36. National Bureau of Statistics of China, "Total Fiscal Revenue/Expenditure and Growth Rate," http://www.stats.gov.cn/tjsj/ndsj/yb2004-c/indexch.htm, accessed January 19, 2006.

37. Karla W. Simon, "Creating an Enabling Legal Environment for Chinese NPOs," testimony for the Congressional-Executive Commission on China hearing *To Serve the People: NGOs and the Development of Civil Society in China*, March 23, 2003, http://www.cecc.gov/pages/roundtables/032403/Simon.php, accessed February 23, 2006.

38. "NGO Management Comes under Review," *China Daily*, December 15, 2005.

39. *Directory of International NGOs in China*, http://www.chinadevelopmentbrief.com/dingo, accessed February 23, 2006.

40. Zhang Ximing, "The Ten Tactics the U.S. Uses in Launching 'Color Revolutions,'" *Liaowang Zhoukan*, December 20, 2005.

41. Amnesty International, "China, 2005," http://web.amnesty.org/report2005/chn-summary-eng, accessed January 12, 2006.

42. "Special Rapporteur on Torture Highlights: Challenges at End of Visit to China," United Nations Press Release, December 2, 2005.

43. "PRC FM Spokesman Says China Willing to Cooperate with UN Rights Reporter," *AFP*, December 5, 2005.

44. U.S. Department of State, "Background Notes: China," http://www.state.gov/r/pa/ei/bgn/18902.htm, accessed January 12, 2006.

45. See the website www.chineseprotestantchurch.org, accessed February 24, 2006.

46. Betty Ann Maheu, "The Catholic Church in China," *America*, vol. 193, no. 14 (November 7, 2005).

47. United States Department of State, *Report on International Religious Freedom 2005*, http://www.state.gov/g/drl/rls/irf/2005, accessed January 12, 2006.

48. See also "Quanmian tuijin yifa xingzheng shishi gangyao" ["Outline for Promoting the Comprehensive Implementation of Administration in Accordance with the Law"], effective March 22, 2004, http://news.xinhuanet.com/zhengfu/2004-04/21/content_ 1431232.htm, accessed February 23, 2006.

49. "Amendments to Improve Petitioner System," *China Daily*, February 24, 2005.

50. "Guowuyuan 2005 fazhi gongzuo zongshu: jiakuai jianshe fazhi zhengfu" ["Summary of Legal Work of the State Council in 2005: Accelerating the Establishment of Law-based Government"], December 29, 2005, http://www.gov.cn/zfjs/2005-12/29/content_ 141063.htm, accessed February 23, 2006.

51. Wu Nanlan, "More Public Hearings Urged," *china.org.cn*, November 1, 2005, http://service.china.org.cn/link/wcm/Show_Text ?info_id=147177&p_qry=people's%20and%20congress%20and%20 system, accessed February 23, 2006.

52. Congressional-Executive Commission on China, *2005 Annual Report*, Part V, http://www.cecc.gov/pages/annualRpt/annualRpt05/ 2005_5e_access.php#6a; He Dawei, et al., "30 Percent of Petitions Stem from Loss of Popular Faith in Legal Justice," *news.xinhuanet. com*, November 29, 2005, http://www.chinalawdigest.com/article. php?aid=527, accessed February 23, 2006.

53. Congressional-Executive Commission on China, "Chinese Courts and Judicial Reform," http://www.cecc.gov/pages/virtual Acad/rol/judreform.php, accessed February 23, 2006.

54. Tim Johnson, "Lawsuits Sprout in China as Interest in Legal Affairs Blooms," *Knight Ridder*, November 12, 2003. China officially reports there were 118,000 certified lawyers at the end of 2004 and 11,691 law firms. "Full Text of White Paper: 'Building of Political Democracy in China,'" *Xinhua*, October 19, 2005, in Open Source Center, CPP20051019078042.

55. "Woguo zhiye lushi da 11.8 wan ren," ["Our Country's Full-time Lawyers Reach 118,000"], *Legal Daily*, June 14, 2005, http://

www.legaldaily.com.cn/bm/2005–06/14/content_154485.htm, accessed February 23, 2006.

56. "Legal Aid Helped 430,000 Chinese in 2005," *Xinhua*, January 11, 2006, http://www.china.org.c/english/2006/Jan/154778.htm, accessed February 23, 2006.

57. Bruce Dickson, "Populist Authoritarianism: The Future of the Chinese Communist Party," paper presented at Carnegie Endowment for International Peace, November 2, 2005, http://www. carnegieendowment.org/events/index.cfm?fa=eventDetail&id=823&& prog=zch, accessed January 12, 2006. See also, Suisheng Zhao, "Political Liberalization Without Democratization: Pan Wei's Proposal for Political Reform," *Journal of Contemporary China* (2003), 333–355.

CHINA IN THE WORLD ECONOMY: OPPORTUNITY OR THREAT?

1. As measured by the sum of imports and exports. China became the globe's third largest importer in 2003.

2. Robert Devlin, Antoni Estevaderodal, and Andres Rodriguez, *The Emergence of China: Opportunities and Challenges for Latin America and the Caribbean* (Washington D.C.: Inter-AmericanDevelopment Bank, forthcoming), http://ddocs.iadb.org/wsdocs/getdocument.aspx ?docnum+447111, accessed February 13, 2006.

3. Scott C. Bradford, Paul L. E. Grieco, and Gary Hufbauer, "The Payoff to America from Global Integration," in C. Fred Bergsten, ed., *The United States and the World Economy: Foreign Economic Policy for the Next Decade*, ed. C. Fred Bergsten, (Washington D.C.: Peterson Institute for International Economics, 2005), 65–109.

4. Kenneth F. Scheve and Matthew J. Slaughter, *Globalization and the Perceptions of American Workers* (Washington D.C.: Peterson Institute for International Economics, 2001).

5. Japan's current account surplus in 2005 was $164 billion.

6. Department of Commerce, *Bureau of Industry and Security Annual Report for FY 2005* (Washington D.C.: Department of Commerce, forthcoming).

7. These calculations ignore the fact that the licensing data are for the 12 months ending September 2005 while the trade data are for calendar year 2005.

8. While the ratio of import duties to the value of imports in China averaged 2.7 percent in 1996–98, the ratios for Argentina, Brazil, India, Indonesia, Mexico, and Turkey, (for slightly varying multiple year periods in the years 1996 through 2002) were 7.8, 8.4, 18.2, 1.2, 1.9, and 1.8 percent, respectively. World Trade Organization, Country Profiles, http://stat.wto.org?CountryProfiles.htm, accessed January 25, 2006.

9. Nicholas R. Lardy, *Integrating China into the Global Economy* (Washington D.C.: Brookings Institution Press, 2002), 75–79.

10. Judith Banister, "Manufacturing Employment and Compensation in China," December 2004. US Department of Labor, Bureau of Labor Statistics, Foreign Labor Statistics, www.bls.gov/fls/China report.pdf, accessed July 20, 2005.

11. Bureau of Labor Statistics, *National Compensation Survey; Employer Costs for Employee Compensation*, March 2005, www.bls.gov/ncs/home.htm#news, accessed November 15, 2005.

12. World Bank, *World Development Indicators 2002* (Washington D.C.: World Bank, 2002), 64–66.

13. Gary Hufbauer and Yee Wong, *China Bashing 2004*, Institute for International Economics Policy Brief 04–5 (Washington D.C.: Peterson Institute for International Economics, 2004), 43.

14. Obviously, a major U.S. recession that massively reduced imports across the board would constitute an exception to this forecast.

15. GDP growth in 2005, according to the official preliminary estimate released in January 2006, moderated only slightly to 9.9 percent compared to 10.1 percent in 2004. However, since the contribution of net exports to growth in 2005 was at an all time high, probably in the neighborhood of one-quarter, domestic investment and/or consumption demand must have slowed significantly. Imports of machinery and equipment in 2005 grew at 15 percent, down sharply from the 31 percent pace of 2004, suggesting that part

of the slowing of domestic demand was due to a slower pace of investment growth.

16. Morris Goldstein and Nicholas Lardy, "Two Stage Currency Reform for China," *Asian Wall Street Journal*, September 12, 2003, A9.

17. Morris Goldstein, "Renminbi Controversies," paper presented at the Cato Institute Conference on Monetary Institutions and Economic Development, November 3, 2005, revised December 2005, available at http://www.iie.com, accessed January 15, 2006.

18. Morris Goldstein and Nicholas Lardy, "A New Way to Deal with the Renminbi," *Financial Times*, January 20, 2006, 13.

19. Michael Mussa, "Sustaining Global Growth while Reducing External Imbalances," in *The United States and the World Economy: Foreign Economic Policy for the Next Decade*, ed. C. Fred Bergsten, 175–207.

20. It should be noted that if other Asian countries were to allow their currencies to appreciate that the overall trade weighted appreciation of the renminbi would be substantially less than its nominal appreciation vis-à-vis the dollar.

21. United States Trade Representative, *2005 Report to Congress on China's WTO Compliance*, December 11, 2005, http://www.ustr.gov, accessed December 12, 2005.

22. Peter K. Yu, "Still Dissatisfied After All These Years: Intellectual Property, Post-WTO China, and the Avoidable Cycle of Futility," Michigan State University College of Law, Legal Studies Research Paper Series, Research Paper No. 03–11, pp. 2–3, http://ssrn.com/abstract=578584, accessed January 26, 2006.

23. "U.S. Official Says Industry More Wary than Government of Bringing WTO Cases Against China," Inside US-China Trade, January 16, 2002, http://www.chinatraddeextra.com/chdsply_txt.asp?f=wto2001.ask&dn=1.16.2002.4.13.13%2, accessed January 17, 2002.

24. Xia Na, "Foreign trademark protected in China," *China Economic News*, no. 30, (August 8, 2005): 3.

25. Ernest H. Preeg, *The Emerging Chinese Advanced Technology Superstate* (Washington D.C.: Manufacturers Alliance and Hudson Institute, 2005).

26. D. Farrell, M. Laboissiere, J. Rosenfeld, S. Sturz, and F. Umezawa, "The Emerging Global Labor Market: Part II—The Supply of Offshore Talent in Services" (McKinsey Global Institute, 2005), 24.

27. Diana Farrell and Andrew J. Grant, "China's Looming Talent Shortage," *McKinsey Quarterly* 2005, no. 4, 56.

28. Calculated on the basis of data in Figure 4.7 and US R&D expenditure of $284.6 billion reported in OECD, *Science and Technology Statistics*, http://www.oecd.org, accessed December 12, 2005.

29. Duke University Master of Engineering Management Program, "Framing the Engineering Outsourcing Debate: Placing the United States on a Level Playing Field with China and India," December 2005, 8, http://memp.pratt.duke.edu/outsourcing, accessed January 6, 2006.

30. Preeg, *The Emerging Chinese Advanced Technology Superstate*, 20.

31. It is a dubious procedure for two reasons. First, since China has not fully participated in the international comparison project of the United Nations, estimates of parities are subject to an unusually large margin of error. Indeed the OECD notes that the "variation in the estimated parities (for China) is extreme." Second, the application of the PPP ratio for overall GDP to R&D expenditures only is questionable since there is no data on relative Chinese prices for research and development expenditures. The ratio could diverge significantly from the economy wide ratio. Two recent studies estimate that for the manufacturing and urban sectors of the Chinese economy the PPP ratio is more than twice the economy wide figure estimated by the World Bank. That suggests that using the World Bank PPP ratio to estimate China's R&D expenditures in PPP dollars results in an overstatement of expenditures of 150 percent. Organization for Economic Cooperation and Development, *China* (Paris: OECD, 2005), 70–71.

32. As if to underscore this point, as this manuscript was going to press the NSF released new estimates of China's high tech imports and exports that are about half the magnitude of the data in Table 4.1. National Science Foundation, *Science and Engineering Indicators 2006*, appendix table 6–4.

33. Mure Dickie, "China's challenge changes the rules of the game," *Financial Times, Special Report, FT Digital Business*, October 19, 2005, 1.

34. George J. Gilboy, "The Myth Behind the Chinese Miracle," *Foreign Affairs* 83, no. 4 (July/August 2004): 40.

35. David Tsent and Jessie Shen, "Asutek set to launch notebook developed entirely by China R&D team," *DigiTimes daily IT news*, December 27, 2005, http://www.digitimes.com/print/a20051226A 2004.html.

36. Korean firms, notably Samsung, also assemble notebook computers in China. Samsung closed its last notebook production plant in Korea in 2005.

37. Jason Dean and Pui-Wing Tam, "The Laptop Trail," *The Wall Street Journal*, June 9, 2005, B1, B8.

38. Value added in processed exports can be calculated from the data the Ministry of Commerce releases annually on processed imports and exports. For example, in 2004 processed exports were $328.0 billion while imports used to produce processed exports, i.e., processing imports, were $221.7 billion, making the value-added ratio equal to 32.4 percent.

39. Semiconductor Industry Association, "Global Semiconductor Sales Hit Record $213 billion in 2004," January 31, 2005, http:// www.sia-online.org, accessed December 10, 2005.

40. General Administration of Customs of the People's Republic of China, *China's Customs Statistics*, no. 12, 2005, 30. Semiconductor Industry Association, "Global Chip Sales Hit Record $227.5 billion in 2005," February 2, 2006, http://www.sia-online.org, accessed February 22, 2006.

41. George J. Gilboy, "The Myth Behind the Chinese Miracle," *Foreign Affairs* 83, no. 4 (July/August 2004): 33–48.

42. Calculation by the National Association of Manufacturers based on data from World Bank and Economy.com.

43. This threshold would have been met sooner but in late 2003 China siphoned off $45 billion of their official foreign exchange reserves to recapitalize two state-owned banks (China Construction Bank and the Bank of China). In 2005, the government injected $15 billion in foreign exchange reserves into the Industrial and Commercial Bank of China in April and $5 billion into the Export-Import Bank of China in July. Then in the fourth quarter of 2005, China's central bank entered into a swap agreement with ten domestic banks to

hold $6 billion in foreign exchange for a one year period. Thus at year-end 2005 China's reported official holdings of foreign exchange stood at $71 billion less than the government's intervention in the foreign exchange markets.

44. Francis E. Warnock and Veronica Cacdac Warnock, "International Capital Flows and U.S. Interest Rates," Board of Governors of the Federal Reserve System, International Finance Discussion Paper No. 840, September 2005, 4.

45. Stephen Green, "CNY appreciation pressure eases as China turns USD bearish," *On The Ground-Asia*, Standard Chartered Bank, January 6, 2006, 2.

46. United Nations Conference on Trade and Development, *World Investment Report 2005*, 303, 306, http://www.unctad.org/en/doc/wir2005-en.pdf, accessed January 3, 2006.

47. Bureau of Economic Analysis, International Economic Accounts, Foreign Direct Investment in the United States, http://www.bea.gov/bea/di/home/direction.intr, accessed January 4, 2006.

48. Flynt Leverett and Jeffrey Bader, "Managing China-U.S. Energy Competition in the Middle East," *Washington Quarterly* 29, no. 1 (Winter 2005–06):193.

49. Leverett and Bader, "Managing China-US Energy Competition in the Middle East," 198.

50. For estimates of the losses imposed on the United States from the creation of various East Asian trade blocs see Robert Scollay and John P. Gilbert, *New Regional Trading Arrangements in the Asia Pacific?* (Washington D.C.: Peterson Institute for International Economics, 2001).

51. For these products the tariffs are to be reduced to a maximum of 20 percent by 2012 and 5 percent by 2018.

52. For further analysis of these options see C. Fred Bergsten, "A New Steering Committee for the World Economy?" in *Reforming the IMF for the 21st Century* ed. Edwin Truman (Washington D.C.: Peterson Institute for International Economics, forthcoming) and Peter B. Kenen, Jeffrey R. Shafer, Nigel Wicks, and Charles Wyplosz, *International Economic and Financial Cooperation: New Issues, New Actors, New Responses*, Geneva Reports on the World Economy 6 (Geneva: International Center for Monetary and Banking Studies, 2004).

53. Unpublished estimate of Gary Hufbauer based on a disaggre-

gation of the estimated $1 trillion annual gain to the United States as a result of trade liberalization since the end of the Second World War. See Bradford, Grieco, and Hufbauer, "The Payoff to America from Global Integration."

CHINA'S FOREIGN AND SECURITY POLICY: PARTNER OR RIVAL?

1. Ministry of Foreign Affairs of the People's Republic of China, *China's Independent Foreign Policy of Peace*, August 18, 2003, http://www.fmprc.gov.cn/eng/wjdt/wjzc/t24881.htm, accessed November 22, 2005.

2. Jiang Zemin's report delivered at the 16th National Congress of the Communist Party of China, November 2002.

3. See: Carola McGiffert, ed., *Chinese Images of the United States* (Washington D.C.: CSIS Press, 2005).

4. Information Office of the State Council of the People's Republic of China, *China's National Defense in 2002* (Beijing: December 2002), http://www.china.org.cn/e-white/20021209/index.htm, accessed December 1, 2005.

5. In October 2006, China formally introduced "harmonious world" to its lexicon for similar reasons of reassurance and to demonstrate its high-minded intentions.

6. Developed by Chinese Premier Zhou Enlai in 1954, the "Five Principles of Peaceful Coexistence" include: mutual respect of sovereignty and territorial integrity; mutual non-aggression; non-interference; equality and mutual benefit; and peaceful coexistence.

7. For instance, China is a participant in formal dialogues with Africa (through the China-Africa Cooperation Forum), the European Union, the Middle East (via the Gulf Cooperation Council), and ASEAN. China was a founding member of the Shanghai Cooperation Organization (SCO) in Central Asia, and serves as an observer at the Organization of American States (OAS) and South Asian Association for Regional Cooperation (SAARC).

8. According to China's White Paper on Peaceful Development, China has canceled about $2 billion in debt from 44 developing countries, provided billions of dollars in preferential loans, and

offers infrastructure, medical, and other types of aid to developing countries. Information Office of the State Council of the People's Republic of China, *China's Peaceful Development Road* (Beijing: December 12, 2005), http://www.china.com.cn/english/features/book/152684.htm, accessed January 5, 2006.

9. Abdulaziz Sager, "Saudi-Chinese relations: Energy first but not last," *The Middle East North Africa Financial Network, Inc. (MENAFN)*, January 23, 2006, http://www.menafn.com/qn_news_story_s.asp?StoryId=122701, accessed February 22, 2006.

10. Robert E. Ebel, *China's Energy Future* (Washington D.C.: CSIS Press, 2005).

11. Bill Gertz, "China builds up strategic sea-lanes," *Washington Times*, January 18, 2005, http://www.washtimes.com/national/2005 0117-115550-1929r.htm, accessed February 20, 2006.

12. Ministry of Commerce of the People's Republic of China, *Top Ten Trading Partners*, February 8, 2006, http://english.mofcom.gov.cn/aarticle/statistic/ie/200602/200602014 68344.html, accessed February 14, 2006.

13. "China-Russia Military Exercise Concludes," *Xinhua News Agency*, August 26, 2005, http://www.ina.org.cn/english/2005/Aug/139796.htm, accessed December 1, 2005.

14. "Full Text of Anti-Secession Law," *People's Daily Online*, March 14, 2005, Article 4, http://english.people.com.cn/200503/14/eng20050314_176746.html, accessed January 25, 2006.

15. Office of the Secretary of Defense, *Annual Report to Congress: The Military Power of the People's Republic of China 2006*, (Washington, D.C.: United States Department of Defense, 2006), 3.

16. Ministry of Commerce of the People's Republic of China, *Top Ten Trading Partners*, February 8, 2006, http://english.mofcom.gov.cn/aarticle/statistic/ie/200602/20060201468344.html, accessed February 14, 2006.

17. "Full Text of Anti-Secession Law," *People's Daily Online*, March 14, 2005, Article 8, http://english.people.com.cn/200503/14/eng20050314_176746.html, accessed January 25, 2006.

18. American Institute in Taiwan, *Taiwan Relations Act*, Section 2b–5, 3a, Public Law 96–8 96th Congress, January 1, 1979, http://www.ait.org.tw/en/about_ait/tra, accessed January 5, 2006.

19. At the same time, Chen's threat to abolish the National Unifi-

cation Council and National Unification Guidelines in February 2006 raised concerns in China about the ability of the United States to constrain Chen, despite its intent. China remains wary that Chen may promote initiatives to distance Taiwan further from the mainland as his term expires in 2008. China's attempts to empower Chen's political opponents, Chen's political weakness, and his desire to demonstrate his continued political viability create the potential for Chen to take such actions in coming years, which has alarmed China—and the United States—and attracted renewed attention to the impact of Chinese tactics and Taiwan domestic politics on future developments across the Taiwan Strait.

20. "Build Towards a Harmonious World of Lasting Peace and Common Prosperity," address by Hu Jintao at UN General Assembly, September 15, 2005.

21. Information Office of the State Council of the People's Republic of China, *China's Peaceful Development Road* (Beijing: December 12, 2005), http://www.china.com.cn/english/features/book/152684.htm, accessed January 3, 2006.

22. "Trade hits record high," *Asia Pulse*, February 23, 2006, http://www.atimes.com/atimes/Japan/HB23Dh03.html, accessed February 23, 2006.

23. Shanghai Huazhong Consulting Service, *Monthly Statistics of 2005*, http://www.shcs.com.cn/cn/economy/pdf/12.Monthly%20Data%20Updated%20(Dec,%202005).pdf, accessed February 20, 2006.

24. If the European Union is counted as a single entity, the EU would be China's largest trade partner, with Japan dropping to third.

25. China and Japan have been engaged in an increasingly tense stand-off over disputed territory in the East China Sea. The disputed area includes the Diaoyutai (Senkaku, in Japanese) islands, and the Chunxiao, Duanqiao, and Tianwaitian (Shirakaba, Kusunoki, and Kashi) oil and gas fields.

26. The Ministry of Foreign Affairs of Japan, *Joint Statement: U.S.-Japan Security Consultative Committee* (Washington, D.C.: February 19, 2005) Article 10, http://www.mofa.go.jpegion/n-america/us/securitycc/joint0502.html, accessed December 1, 2005.

27. Pyongyang's missile tests on July 5, 2006, conducted despite China's private messages of opposition, highlighted Beijing's limited influence and growing frustration with Pyongyang. As a result,

Beijing supported a UN resolution criticizing the North, although it resisted a harsher measure imposing sanctions.

28. Charles Krauthammer, "China's Moment," *Washington Post*, September 23, 2005, http://www.washingtonpost.com/wp-dyn/content/article/2005/09/22/AR2005092202257.html, accessed January 10, 2006.

29. For instance, a Japanese newspaper reported in March 2006 that North Korea planned to develop Bidan Island along its border with China into a special economic zone as an experiment in economic engagement with the outside world. The establishment of special economic zones in China were early hallmarks of its "reform and opening up" policy during the 1980s. "N. Korea to Setup Special Economic Zone Near China," *Chosun Ilbo*, March 7, 2006, http://english.chosun.com/w21data/html/news/200603/200603070028.html, accessed March 7, 2006.

30. Bilateral trade exceeded $100 billion for the first time in 2005. South Korea enjoys a $20 billion trade surplus. The ROK has become China's sixth largest trade partner and fourth largest foreign investor. Ministry of Commerce of the People's Republic of China, *Top Ten Trading Partners*, February 8, 2006, http://english.moom.gov.cn/a article/statistic/ie/200602/20060201468344.html, accessed February 14, 2006; Shanghai Huazhong Consulting Service, *Monthly Statistics of 2005*, http://www.shcs.com.cn/cn/economy/pdf/12.Monthly%20Data %20Updated%20(Dec,%202005).pdf, accessed February 20, 2006.

31. The U.S. Department of Defense has been issuing annual reports to Congress on China's military power since 1997.

32. Information Office of the State Council of the People's Republic of China, *China's National Defense in 2004* (Beijing: December 2004), http://www.china.org.cn/e-white/20041227/index.htm, accessed December 1, 2005.

33. "China's defense budget up 14.7% in 2006," *Xinhua*, March 4, 2006.

34. Information Office of the State Council of the People's Republic of China, *China's National Defense in 2004* (Beijing: December 2004), http://www.china.org.cn/e-white/20041227/index.htm, accessed December 1, 2005.

35. Ibid.

Authors

C. Fred Bergsten has been director of the Peter G. Peterson Institute for International Economics since its creation in 1981. He has been the most widely quoted think-tank economist in the world over the eight-year period 1997–2005, was ranked in the top 50 "Who Really Move the Markets?" by *Fidelity Investment's Worth*, and was cited as "one of the ten people who can change your life" in *USA Today*.

Dr. Bergsten was assistant secretary for international affairs of the U.S. Treasury during 1977–81. He also functioned as undersecretary for monetary affairs during 1980–81, representing the United States on the G-5 Deputies and in preparing G-7 summits. During 1969–71, Dr. Bergsten coordinated U.S. foreign economic policy in the White House as assistant for international economic affairs to Dr. Henry Kissinger at the National Security Council. Dr. Bergsten was chairman of the Eminent Persons Group of the Asia Pacific Economic Cooperation (APEC) forum from 1993 to 1995, authoring its three reports that recommended "free and open trade in the region by 2010 and 2020" as adopted at the APEC summits in 1993 and 1994. He was also chairman of the Competitiveness Policy Council created by the Congress from 1991 through 1995.

Dr. Bergsten has authored, coauthored, or edited 36 books on international economic issues. He has received the Exceptional Service Award of the Treasury Department and the Legion d'Honneur from the Government of France, and was named an honorary fellow of the Chinese Academy of Social Sciences in 1997. Dr. Bergsten received MA, MALD, and Ph.D. degrees from the Fletcher School of Law and Diplomacy and a BA magna cum laude and honorary Doctor of Humane Letters from Central Methodist College.

Bates Gill holds the Freeman Chair in China Studies at CSIS. He previously served as a senior fellow in Foreign Policy Studies and inaugural director of the Center for Northeast Asian Policy Studies at the Brookings Institution. In 1992–93, he held the Fei Yiming Chair in Comparative Politics at the Johns Hopkins University Center for Chinese and American Studies, Nanjing, China.

His current research examines China's domestic social, economic, and political transformation, including a focus on the country's looming HIV/AIDS challenge. He is the author of three books and co-editor of two others, including the forthcoming, *Rising Star: China's New Security Diplomacy*. He has recently published his work in *Foreign Affairs*, *Survival*, and *National Interest*, and in the *International Herald Tribune*, the *New York Times*, the *Washington Post*, and the *Washington Times*.

Dr. Gill serves on the boards of the National Committee on United States-China Relations, the U.S.-China Policy Foundation, the American Association for Chinese Studies, the Feris Foundation of America, and the China-Merck HIV/AIDS Public Private Partnership, and is a senior advisor to the U.S.-Asia Institute. He is also on the editorial boards of the *Journal of Contemporary China*, the *Hong Kong Journal*, and *China Security*. He is a member of the Council on Foreign Relations and the International Institute of Strategic Studies. Dr. Gill received his Ph.D. in foreign affairs from the University of Virginia.

Nicholas R. Lardy is a senior fellow at the Peter G. Peterson Institute for International Economics and is considered one of the world's leading experts on the Chinese economy. Dr. Lardy came to the Institute in March 2003 from the Brookings Institution, where he had been a senior fellow in the Foreign Policy Studies Program since 1995. From 1997–2000, he was also the Frederick Frank Adjunct Professor of International Trade and Finance at the Yale University School of Management. Prior to his work at Brookings, Dr. Lardy served at the University of Washington from 1983–1995, including as director of the Henry M. Jackson School of International Studies (1991–1995) and as chair of the China Program (1984–1989), among other posts. He was an assistant and associate professor of economics at Yale University from 1975–1983.

Dr. Lardy's publications include *Prospects for a U.S.-Taiwan Free Trade Agreement* (with Daniel H. Rosen) (IIE: 2004); *Integrating China into the Global Economy* (Brookings Press, 2002); and *China's Unfinished Economic Revolution* (Brookings Press, 1998).

Dr. Lardy serves on the Board of Directors and Executive Committee of the National Committee on United States–China Relations; is a member of the Council on Foreign Relations; and is a member of the editorial boards of *The China Quarterly*, *Journal of Asian Business*, *China Review*, and *China Economic Review*. He received his BA from the University of Wisconsin in 1968 and his Ph.D. from the University of Michigan in 1975, both in economics.

Derek J. Mitchell is senior fellow for Asia in the CSIS International Security Program, where he manages all Asia-related studies. Prior to joining CSIS in 2001, Mr. Mitchell was special assistant for Asian and Pacific Affairs, Office of the Secretary of Defense, from 1997–2001, when he served alternately as senior country director for China, Taiwan, Mongolia, and Hong Kong (2000–1), director for regional security affairs (1998–2000), country director for Japan (1997–8), and senior country director for the Philippines, Indonesia, Malaysia, Brunei, and Singapore (1998–9). Mr. Mitchell was the principal author of the Defense Department's 1998 East Asia Strategy Report. He received the "Office of the Secretary of Defense Award for Exceptional Public Service" in January 2001.

Prior to joining the Pentagon, Mr. Mitchell served as senior program officer for Asia and the former Soviet Union at the National Democratic Institute for International Affairs in Washington, D.C. From 1993–1997, Mr. Mitchell developed the Institute's long-term approach to Asia, and worked on democratic development programs in Armenia, Burma, Cambodia, Georgia,

Pakistan, and Thailand. From 1988–1989, Mr. Mitchell worked as an editor and reporter at the *China Post* in Taiwan. From 1986 to 1988, he served in the foreign policy office of Senator Edward M. Kennedy.

Mr. Mitchell received his MA from the Fletcher School of Law and Diplomacy. Mr. Mitchell studied Chinese language at Nanjing University, PRC, and is a regular print, radio, and television commentator on East Asian security issues.

Organizations

THE CENTER FOR STRATEGIC AND INTERNATIONAL STUDIES

CSIS seeks to advance global security and prosperity in an era of economic and political transformation by providing strategic insights and practical policy solutions to decision makers. CSIS serves as a strategic planning partner for government by conducting research and analysis and developing policy initiatives that look into the future and anticipate change.

Founded in 1962 by David M. Abshire and Admiral Arleigh Burke, CSIS is a bipartisan, nonprofit organization headquartered in Washington, D.C. with more than 220 full-time staff and a large network of affiliated experts. Former U.S. senator Sam Nunn became chairman of the CSIS Board of Trustees in 1999, and John J. Hamre has led CSIS as its president and chief executive officer since April 2000.

CSIS experts conduct research and analysis and develop policy initiatives that are organized around more than 25 programs grouped under three themes: defense and security, global challenges, and regional transformation.

With one of the most comprehensive programs on U.S. defense policy and international security, CSIS proposes reforms to U.S. defense organization, security policy, and the defense industrial and technology base. Other CSIS programs offer solutions to the challenges of proliferation, transnational terrorism, homeland security, and post-conflict reconstruction.

With programs on demographics and population, energy security, global health, technology, and the international financial and economic system, CSIS addresses the new drivers of risk and opportunity on the world stage.

Finally, CSIS is the only institution of its kind with resident experts studying the transformation of all of the world's major geographic regions. CSIS specialists seek to anticipate changes in key countries and regions—from Africa to Asia, from Europe to Latin America, and from the Middle East to North America.

THE PETER G. PETERSON INSTITUTE FOR INTERNATIONAL ECONOMICS

The Institute is the only major research institution in the United States devoted to international economic issues. Since 1981, the Institute has provided timely, objective analysis and concrete solutions to key international economic problems. It has been called "the most influential think tank on the planet."

The Institute attempts to anticipate emerging issues and to be ready with practical ideas to inform and shape public debate. Its audience includes government officials and legislators, business and labor leaders, management and staff at international organizations, university-based scholars and their students, other research institutions and nongovernmental organizations, the media, and the public at large. It addresses these groups both in the United States and around the world.

The Institute's staff of about 50 includes more than two dozen researchers, who are conducting about 30 studies at any given time. Its agenda emphasizes global macroeconomic topics, international money and finance, trade and related social issues, investment, and the international implications of new technologies. Current priority is attached to China, globalization and the backlash against it, outsourcing, reform of the international financial architecture, and new trade negotiations at the multilateral, regional, and bilateral levels. Institute staff and research cover all key regions—especially Asia, Europe, the Middle East, and Latin America as well as the United States itself. In late 2001, the Institute helped create the Center for Global Development to address poverty and development issues in the poor countries. Dr. C. Fred Bergsten has been director of the Institute throughout its initial quarter century.

Institute studies have helped provide the intellectual foundation for many of the major international financial initiatives of the past two decades: reform of the IMF, adoption of international banking standards, exchange rate systems in the G-7 and emerging-market economies, policies toward the dollar and the euro as well as the Chinese renminbi and other Asian currencies, and responses to debt and currency crises. The Institute has made important contributions to key trade policy decisions, including fast-track legislation and related Trade Adjustment Assistance reforms, the Doha and Uruguay Rounds and the development of the WTO, NAFTA and other U.S. free trade agreements, APEC and East Asian regionalism, a series of United States–Japan negotiations, reform of sanctions policy, liberalization of U.S. export controls and export credits, and specific measures such as PNTR for China in 2000 and the abolition of special protection for steel in 2004. Other influential analyses have addressed economic reform in Europe, Latin America, and Japan, globalization and policy responses to it, outsourcing, energy policy, electronic commerce, corruption, foreign direct investment both into and out of the United States, global warming and international environmental policy, and key sectors such as agriculture, financial services, steel, telecommunications, and textiles.

Acknowledgements

The authors express their great appreciation to the following people for their support of the China Balance Sheet project.

Project co-chairs: C. Fred Bergsten and John J. Hamre
Advisory committee: see following list
Senior advisor: Ben W. Heineman, Jr.
Project advisor: J. Bradford Jensen
Project executive director: Carola McGiffert
Editorial advisor: Vinca LaFleur
Contributing authors: Robert Ebel, Jamie Horsley, Jikun Huang, Keith Maskus, Daniel H. Rosen, Scott Rozelle, Anne Thurston, and Jennifer Turner
Research associates: Chietigj Bajpaee, Giwon Jeong, Xiaoqing Lu, and Melissa Murphy
Publication team: Peter Osnos, founder and editor-at-large of PublicAffairs, and the staff, particularly Melissa Raymond, Nina D'Amario, Whitney Peeling, Lisa Kaufman, Clive Priddle, consultant Gene Taft, and designer Jane Raese

Advisory Committee

We have been fortunate to be able to draw on the extensive knowledge of a remarkable group of experts on China and U.S.-China relations, representing a range of perspectives. Many of these advisors participated in brainstorming meetings or provided comments on draft versions of this volume, and we are deeply grateful for their guidance and support. However, the findings and opinions expressed in this book solely reflect those of the authors. They do not necessarily represent the views of our advisors or other supporters.

Among those from whom we solicited views are:

Jonathan Anderson
Jeffrey A. Bader
Charlene Barshefsky
Doug Bereuter
Samuel R. Berger
Dennis Blair
Pieter Bottelier
Richard C. Bush
Kurt M. Campbell
Richard N. Cooper
Bruce Dickson
Thomas E. Donilon
Michael P. Dooley
Robert Ebel
Elizabeth Economy
James V. Feinerman
William W. Ferguson

Joseph Fewsmith III
David M. Finkelstein
Charles W. Freeman
Michael Gadbaw
Paul Gewirtz
Bonnie Glaser
Morris Goldstein
Michael Goltzman
Thomas Gottschalk
Maurice Greenberg
Scott Hallford
Carol Hamrin
Harry Harding
Ben W. Heineman, Jr.
David Henson
Carla A. Hills
Richard Holbrooke

Jamie Horsley
Janet Howard
Richard Jackson
L. Oakley Johnson
James A. Kelly
Henry Kissinger
William Lane
Lawrence J. Lau
Malcolm Lee
Cheng Li
Kenneth Lieberthal
James R. Lilley
Xiaobo Lu
Keith Maskus
Michael McDevitt
Eric A. McVadon
Evan Medeiros
R. Scott Miller
T. James Min II
G. Mustafa Mohatarem
Peter Morici
James C. Mulvenon
Kevin G. Nealer
Paul Neureiter
Matt Niemeyer
Marcus Noland
Minxin Pei

Dwight H. Perkins
Ernest H. Preeg
Clyde Prestowitz
Jean D. Pritchard
Thomas G. Rawski
William A. Reinsch
Stephen Roach
Alan D. Romberg
Daniel H. Rosen
J. Stapleton Roy
Scott Rozelle
James Sasser
Phillip C. Saunders
Randy Schriver
Elizabeth Nash Schwartz
Jeffery R. Shafer
David Shambaugh
Anne Solomon
Michael D. Swaine
Murray Scott Tanner
Frederick Telling
Anne F. Thurston
Jennifer L. Turner
Arthur Waldron
Stephen J. Yates
Shirley Zebroski

Index

ACFTA. *See* ASEAN-China
free trade area
Administrative Licensing Law,
67
Administrative Litigation Law
(ALL), 67
Administrative Penalties Law
(APL), 67
Advanced technology products
(ATP), 100, 104
Aging
in China, 22, 46–48
in U.S., 76
Agreement on Trade in Goods,
114
Agriculture, 22
in China, 23, 36–37
in European Union, 129
labor in, 23
in U.S., 129
AIDS. *See* HIV/AIDS
Aksai Chin, 121
ALL. *See* Administrative
Litigation Law
America. *See* U.S.
American Electronics
Association, 100
Amnesty International, 63, 64
Angola, 132

Anti-Secession Law, 133, 135,
137
APEC. *See* Asia Pacific
Economic Cooperation
APL. *See* Administrative
Penalties Law
Apparel industry, 74, 99
in U.S., 11
Argentina, 132
income gap in, 30–31
tariffs in, 83
Arrests, 43
Arunachel Pradesh, 121
ASEAN. *See* Association of
Southeast Asian Nations
ASEAN + 3, 126, 133
ASEAN-China free trade area
(ACFTA), 114
Asia Pacific Economic
Cooperation (APEC), 123
Asian Monetary Facility, 12
Association of Southeast Asian
Nations (ASEAN), 114,
123, 126, 133, 134, 177
Asutek Computer, 106
ATP. *See* Advanced technology
products
Australia, 114
Avian flu, 7, 52, 158

Bader, Jeff, 113
Bangladesh, 130
   income gap in, 31
Bank of America, 25
Bank of China, 25, 175
Bankruptcy
   in China, 23, 24, 38
   of state-owned companies, 38
Banks, 4, 20, 25, 29, 175, 176.
      See also World Bank
Beijing University, 51
Belgrade, bombing in, 122
Best Buy, 81
Birthrate, 47
Bolivia, 132
Brazil, 132, 160
   income gap in, 30–31
   tariffs in, 81, 83
Brookings Institution, 113
Brunei, 115
Buddhists, 66
Budget deficits, 76
Burma, 13, 115, 130, 132, 141,
      158
Bush, George W., 27, 96, 122,
      132

C4ISR (command, control,
      communications, computer,
      information, surveillance,
      and reconnaissance), 151
Cambodia, 115
Catholic Church, 66
CCB. *See* China Construction
      Bank
CCP. *See* Chinese Communist
      Party

CD players, 105
Central Committee. *See*
      Chinese Communist Party
      Central Committee
Central Discipline Inspection
      Commission, 44
Central Economic Work
      Conference, 26
Central Military Commission,
      58
Century of humiliation, 118, 119
CFIUS. *See* Committee on
      Foreign Investment in the
      United States (CFIUS)
Chechnya, 134
Chen Shui-bian, 136, 178–179
Chiang Kai-Shek, 135
Chile, 132
   income gap in, 30–31
China
   abortion in, 48–49
   aging of, 22, 46–48
   agriculture in, 23, 36–37
   avian flu in, 7, 52, 158
   bankruptcy in, 23, 24, 38
   banks in, 4, 25, 29
   birthrate in, 47
   Christianity in, 7, 59, 65–66
   civil rights in, 62–66, 133
   corruption in, 43–45
   currency and, 12, 29, 80,
      90–95, 109
   current account position in,
      82
   deforestation in, 54
   developing world and, 13,
      21, 121, 129, 141, 159

diseases in, 9
drugs in, 9
economy of, 2, 3, 18, 73
education in, 50–51, 103, 167
elections in, 58–59
employment in, 32
energy in, 34–35
environment of, 34
European Union and, 132
exports from, 10
fiber optics in, 153
fiscal challenges of, 37–38
fiscal policy in, 25–26
folk religions and, 7–8
foreign direct investment in, 4
foreign exchange reserves of, 4, 7
foreign policy of, 12–13, 118
foreign-owned companies in, 21, 89, 105
gender imbalance in, 47–49
health care in, 27, 38–39, 52, 164
high technology in, 99, 102, 174
highways in, 103
HIV/AIDS in, 6, 52, 62, 158
human rights in, 133
import licensing in, 84
imports in, 86, 171, 172
income gap in, 4–5, 6, 30
India and, 121, 128
infanticide in, 49
Internet in, 7, 64–65, 71
investment in, 19, 21
Israel and, 153

Japan and, 114, 142
joint ventures in, 21, 89, 105
labor in, 21–22, 23, 46–48, 87–89
land confiscation in, 41, 42
Latin America and, 33, 119, 129, 132
lawyers in, 8, 69–70, 170
life expectancy in, 18, 47, 51
literacy in, 18, 22, 50
migration in, 7, 19, 32, 46
military in, 5, 14, 149, 150
missiles and, 136
mobile phones in, 7
monetary policy in, 25–26
natural resources and, 13, 33
nongovernmental organizations in, 7, 50, 55, 61, 62, 71, 123
North Korea and, 145
oil and, 33, 35–36, 111, 112, 130, 131, 134, 157
one-child policy in, 47
patents in, 95, 96, 98
pensions in, 53
per capita incomes in, 4, 9
politics of, 3, 5
pollution in, 6, 53–54
population of, 15, 32, 45, 46–48
poverty in, 18, 163
private property in, 107
research and development in, 100, 101, 103, 174
Russia and, 126, 128, 134, 152
SARS in, 7

China (*continued*)
  savings in, 21, 28
  sex trade in, 52
  shipbuilding in, 153
  social services in, 38
  social unrest in, 6, 7, 40
  Southeast Asia and, 12, 114, 120–121, 123, 133–134
  South Korea and, 148, 180
  space program in, 153
  state-owned firms in, 23, 24
  stock market in, 25
  students in, 4
  tariffs in, 83, 85
  taxes in, 27
  territorial claims of, 15
  torture in, 63
  trade barriers in, 11, 81
  trade by, 3, 102
  trade surplus of, 4, 10, 26, 78, 79, 90, 171–172
  urbanization in, 31–32, 46
  U.S. bonds and, 108
  U.S. companies and, 10
  as U.S. trading partner, 17
  vehicle ownership in, 54
  wages in, 79, 87–89
  water in, 54–55
China Construction Bank (CCB), 25, 175
China Democracy Party, 7
China National Offshore Oil Corporation (CNOOC), 75, 110, 112, 113, 130
China-Africa Cooperation Forum, 177

Chinese Academy of Social Sciences, 41, 60
Chinese Communist Party (CCP), 8, 26, 44, 45, 56, 57–58, 60, 71, 72, 119, 123, 135, 142
Chinese Communist Party Central Committee, 27, 34, 42
Chinese Ministry of Health, 52
Chinese Ministry of Labor and Social Security, 53
Chinese Ministry of Science and Technology, 104
Christianity, 7, 59, 65–66. *See also* Patriotic Christian Churches
Circuit City, 81
Civil rights, 62–66, 133
Climate change. *See* Global warming
Clinton, Bill, 76
CNOOC. *See* China National Offshore Oil Corporation
Command, control, communications, computer, information, surveillance, and reconnaissance. *See* C4ISR
Committee on Foreign Investment in the United States (CFIUS), 113
Compal, 106
Computers. *See* Notebook computers; Personal computers

Copyrights, 95
Corruption, 43–45
Corruption Perception Index, 43
Counterfeiting, of trademarks, 96, 97
Counterterrorism. *See* Terrorism
Crime
  international, 1
  organized, 9, 157
Cuba, 132
Currencies, 173. *See also* Renminbi
  of Asian countries, 109
  China and, 12, 29, 80, 109
  exchange rate with, 93
  pegging of, 93–94
  problems with, 92–95
  undervaluation of, 90–92
Cyberdissidents, 65

Darfur, 141
Defense White Paper, 126, 149, 151
Deforestation, 54
Democracy
  in China, 3
  in Indonesia, 71
  inner-Party, 58
  in Iraq, 71
  participatory, 56
  in Russia, 71
  in Taiwan, 71
Democratic Progressive Party (DPP), 136

Demography. *See* Population
Deng Xiaoping, 31, 60, 73, 118
Diaoyutai islands, 121, 179
Digital cameras, 105
Diseases, 1, 140, 157, 158
  avian flu, 7, 52, 158
  in China, 9
  HIV/AIDS, 6, 52, 62, 158
  SARS, 7
  tuberculosis, 7
Dispute Settlement Body, 96
Doha Round, 115, 129
DPP. *See* Democratic Progressive Party
Drugs, 157
  in China, 9
  trafficking in, 139
DVD players, 105

East Asia Summit, 14, 133
EBay, 97
Economy
  in China, 2, 3, 18, 73
  in Japan, 23
  in U.S., 3, 76
Education
  in China, 50–51, 103, 167
  in European Union, 132
  in U.S., 10–11
Elections, 58–59
Eleventh Five-Year Program, 26–27, 34, 42
  environment and, 55
Employment
  in China, 32
  in U.S., 76

Energy, 157–158. *See also*
    International Energy
    Agency; Oil
  in China, 34–35, 121
  prices of, 77
Entertainment. *See* Recorded
    entertainment
Environment. *See also* Pollution
  conservation of, 34
  degradation of, 1
EP-3 spy plane incident, 122
EU. *See* European Union
European Union (EU), 64, 115,
    160, 177
  agriculture in, 129
  China and, 132
  education in, 132
Exchange rates, 93
Exon-Florio Bill, 110
Export licensing, 80
Export-Import Bank of China,
    175
Exports
  from China, 10
  licensing of, 80
  processed, 90
  of U.S., 89

Falun Gong, 7, 66
FBI, 123
Federal Reserve, 109–110
Fiber optics, 153
Financial Times, 24
First International Computer,
    106
Fiscal policy, 25–26

Five Principles of Peaceful
    Coexistence, 129, 177
Folk religions, 7–8
Footwear, 74, 99
Foreign-owned companies, 21,
    89, 105
Framework Agreement for
    Overall Economic
    Cooperation, 114
Free trade agreements (FTAs),
    114, 115
Freedom House, 64
FTAs. *See* Free trade
    agreements
Fudan University, 51
Furniture industry, 74

G-4, 116
G-7, 116
G-20, 116
Gender imbalance, 47–49
Georgia, 61
Germany, 89
Gilboy, George J., 107
Global warming, 158
Globalization, 11
  backlash against, 77
Goldstein, Morris, 93
Gulf Cooperation Council, 177
Gulf War. *See* Iraq War

Haier, 110
Health care. *See also* World
    Health Organization
  in China, 27, 38–39, 52, 164
  in U.S., 10–11

High technology, 99, 102, 174
Highways, 103
HIV/AIDS, 6, 52, 62, 158
Hong Kong, 90, 119
Hu Angang, 32
Hu Jintao, 57, 58, 60, 63, 96
Huang Ju, 57
Human rights. *See* Civil rights
Human Rights Watch 2005, 64

IBM, 110
IEA. *See* International Energy
    Agency
Illiteracy. *See* Literacy
IMF. *See* International
    Monetary Fund
Import licensing, 84
Imports, 86, 171, 172
Income gap
    in Argentina, 30–31
    in Bangladesh, 31
    in Brazil, 30–31
    in Chile, 30–31
    in China, 4–5, 6, 30
    in India, 31
    in Indonesia, 31
    in U.S., 77
India, 74, 160
    China and, 121, 128
    income gap in, 31
    tariffs in, 81, 83
Indonesia
    ASEAN and, 115
    democracy in, 71
    income gap in, 31
    tariffs in, 81, 83

Industrial and Commercial
    Bank of China, 25,
    175–176
Infanticide, 49
Infectious diseases. *See* Diseases
Information technology, 14
Inner-Party democracy, 58
Intel, 106
Intellectual property (IPR), 11,
    95, 107
    violations of, 98
International Energy Agency
    (IEA), 33, 113
International Monetary Fund
    (IMF), 12, 115
Internet
    in China, 7, 64, 71
    policing of, 64–65
Investment, 19, 21
IPR. *See* Intellectual property
IPR Leading Group, 96
Iran, 13, 113, 130, 158
Iraq, 71
Iraq War, 141, 149
Israel, 132, 153

Japan, 11, 17, 33, 73, 90, 96,
    126
    advantages of, 108
    aggression of, 142
    China and, 114, 142
    economy in, 23
    investment in, 24
    Taiwan and, 143
    trade surplus of, 10
    U.S. and, 76

Jia Qinglin, 57
Jiang Zemin, 58, 60
Joint Commission on
    Commerce and Trade, 96
Joint ventures, 21, 89, 105

K2. *See* Karshi-Khanabad
Karimov, Islam, 131
Karshi-Khanabad (K2), 131
Kashi oil field, 179
Kazakhstan, 126
Kim Jong II, 146
Kissinger, Henry, 143
KMT. *See* Kuomintang
Koizumi, Junichiro, 142
Korean War, 146
Kuomintang (KMT), 136
Kusunoki oil field, 179
Kyrgyzstan, 126
    revolution in, 61

Labor. *See also* Employment
    in agriculture, 23
    in China, 21–22, 46–48, 87–89
    literacy and, 22
    productivity of, 88
    wages of, 74
Land
    confiscation of, 41, 42
    deforestation, 54
    degradation of, 54
Laos, 115
Lardy, Nicholas, 93
Latin America, 18, 32–33
Lawyers, 8, 69–70, 170
Lenovo, 110

Leverett, Flynt, 113
Li Changchun, 57
Life expectancy, 18, 47, 51
Literacy, 18
    in China, 22, 50
    labor and, 22
Luo Gan, 57

Ma Jun, 55
Macao, 119
Macedonia, 119–120
Malaysia, 115
Mao Tse-tung, 143
Market forces, 19, 20
Marxism, 60
Mass group incidents, 40
Maytag, 110
McKinsey Global Institute, 103
Mexico, 74
    tariffs in, 81, 83
Microprocessors, 88, 106–107
Microsoft, 106
Migration
    in China, 7, 19, 32, 46
    restrictions on, 19
Military, 5, 149, 150
    information technology and,
        14
Ministry of Commerce, 175
Ministry of Education, 50
Ministry of Foreign Affairs, 160
Ministry of Information
    Industry, 64
Ministry of Justice, 70
Ministry of Public Security, 41,
    64

Ministry of Water Resources, 56
Missiles, 136, 152
Mobile phones, 7, 105
Monetary policy, 25–26
Movies, 96
Music, 96
Muslims, 66

National Association of Manufacturers, 175
National Bureau of Statistics, 163
National Defense Program Outline, 144
National Development and Reform Commission, 160
National Offshore Oil Company, 10
National People's Congress (NPC), 44, 56, 68
National Population and Family Planning Commission, 46
National Reform and Development Commission, 34
National Science Foundation (NSF), 100, 104, 174
National Unification Council, 178–179
National Unification Guidelines, 179
NATO, 134
New Left, 60
New Security Concept, 126
New Zealand, 115

NGOs. See Nongovernmental organizations
Nigeria, 130
Nixon, Richard, 143
Nongovernmental organizations (NGOs), 7, 50, 55, 61, 62, 71, 123
North Korea
    economic zone in, 180
    nuclear weapons in, 123, 145, 147, 148
Notebook computers, 90, 105, 106, 175
NPC. See National People's Congress
NSF. See National Science Foundation
Nuclear weapons. See Weapons
Nujiang River, 43

OAS. See Organization of American States
OECD. See Organization for Economic Co-operation and Development
Oil
    in China, 33, 35–36, 111, 112, 130, 131, 134, 157
    fields, 179
    price of, 35
    Russia and, 134
    U.S. and, 112
Okinawa, 143
Olympic Games, 122
One Country, Two Systems, 135

One-child policy, 47
Organization for Economic
    Co-operation and
    Development (OECD), 74,
    174
Organization of American
    States (OAS), 177
Organized crime, 9, 157

Pakistan, 130
Palestine, 132
Paracel Islands, 121
Partnership for Peace, 134
Party Central Propaganda
    Department, 62
Patents, 95, 98
    infringement on, 96
Patriotic Christian Churches, 65
Pegging, of currency, 93–94
Pensions, 53
People, trafficking in, 9, 157
People's Armed Police, 150
People's Bank of China, 20
People's Congress (PC), 68
People's First Party (PFP), 136
People's Liberation Army
    (PLA), 14–15, 149, 151, 152
Personal computers, 99
PFP. See People's First Party
Pharmaceuticals, 96
Philippines, 115, 132
Piracy, 97, 139
    of recorded entertainment,
    95–96
    of software, 95
PLA. See People's Liberation
    Army

Policy lending, 19
Pollution, 9, 53–54, 157
Population, 15, 45, 46–48. See
    also One-child policy
    increases in, 32
    of U.S., 76
Poverty, 163
PPP. See Purchasing power
    parity
Private property, 107
Privatization, 23
Processed exports, 90
Proliferation Security Initiative,
    147
Protectionism, 12
Purchasing power parity (PPP),
    163, 174
Pyongyang
    missile tests, 179–180

Quanta, 106

Recorded entertainment, piracy
    of, 95–96, 105
Religion. See Buddhists;
    Christianity; Folk religions;
    Religious freedom
Religious freedom, 65. See also
    Civil rights
Renminbi, 90, 92, 93, 109, 173
Reporters Without Borders, 64
Republic of China. See Taiwan
Republic of Korea (ROK). See
    South Korea
Research and development, 4,
    100, 101, 103, 174
Revolution, 61

Roh Moo-hyun, 148
ROK. *See* South Korea
    (Republic of Korea)
Rural Cooperative Medical
    Scheme, 164
Russia, 126, 128
    China and, 134, 152
    democracy in, 71
    weapons and, 134

SAARC. *See* South Asian
    Association for Regional
    Cooperation
SAIC. *See* State Administration
    of Industry and Commerce
Samsung, 175
SARS, 7
Savings
    in China, 21, 28
    in U.S., 28
SCL. *See* State Compensation
    Law
Security Council, 141
Semiconductors, 88, 106–107
Senkaku islands, 121, 179
SEPA. *See* State Environmental
    Protection Agency
Sex selective abortion, 48–49
Sex trade, 52
Shanghai Cooperation
    Organization (SCO), 14,
    126, 131, 177
Shipbuilding, 153
Shirakaba islands, 179
Short-range ballistic missile
    (SRBM), 152
Silk Alley, 97

Singapore, 115
Sino-Japanese War, 119
Six Party talks, 123, 147
Sixteenth Party Congress, 58
Social services, 38
Software, 96
    piracy of, 95
South Asian Association for
    Regional Cooperation
    (SAARC), 177
South Korea, 33, 90, 126
    China and, 148, 180
    FTAs and, 115
    investment in, 24
    notebook computers and, 106
Soviet Union, 56, 59
Space program, 153
Sporting goods, 99
Spratly Islands, 121
SRBM. *See* Short-range ballistic
    missile
State Administration of Industry
    and Commerce (SAIC), 99
State Compensation Law
    (SCL), 67
State Council, 34, 46, 56, 58, 59
State Council Development
    Research Center, 51
State Environmental Protection
    Agency (SEPA), 54, 56
State Price Commission, 19
State Secrets Bureau, 64
Stock market, 25
Strait of Malacca, 130
Submarines, 144, 152
Sudan, 13, 113, 130, 132, 141, 158
Supreme People's Court, 69, 96

Supreme People's
    Procuratorate, 96
Switzerland, 96

Taiwan, 5, 14, 15, 33, 90, 119,
    127, 134, 135, 158, 178
  democracy in, 71
  investment in, 24
  Japan and, 143
  military and, 153–154
  missiles and, 136
  national identity of, 15
  notebook computers and, 106
  unification with, 13, 15
  U.S. and, 123, 127, 138–139
Taiwan Relations Act (TRA),
    137
Tajikistan, 126
Taoism, 66
Target, 81
Tariff rate quota (TRQ), 84
Tariffs, 176
  ACFTA and, 114
  in Argentina, 83
  in Brazil, 81, 83
  in China, 83, 85
  in India, 81, 83
  in Indonesia, 81, 83
  in Mexico, 81, 83
  in Turkey, 83
Taxes, 27
Terrorism, 1, 123, 124–125,
    130, 139–140, 156
TFR. See Total fertility rate
Thailand, 115
Thomson SA, 111

Three Gorges Dam, 58
Tiananmen Square, 119, 133,
    153
Tibet, 63, 65, 119
Tibet Information Network, 65
Tiffany, 97
Torture, 63
Total fertility rate (TFR), 47
Toys, 99
TRA. See Taiwan Relations Act
Trade, 3, 102
  barriers, 11, 81
  secrets, 96
  surplus, 4, 10, 26, 78, 79, 90,
    171–172
Trade deficit, 79
  between U.S. and China, 78
Trademark Law, 95
Trademarks, 95
  in China, 98–99
  counterfeiting of, 96, 97
Trade-Related Aspects of
    Intellectual Property
    Rights (TRIPS), 95, 96
Trafficking
  in drugs, 9, 139, 157
  in people, 9, 157
  in weapons, 9, 157
Transparency International, 43
TRIPS. See Trade-Related
    Aspects of Intellectual
    Property Rights
TRQ. See Tariff rate quota
Tsinghua University, 51
Turkey, 74
  tariffs in, 83

Ukraine, 61
Unemployment. *See*
    Employment
United Nations, 139, 140, 174,
    180. *See also* Security
    Council
United Nations Development
    Program, 53
United Nations International
    Covenant on Civil and
    Political Rights, 63
United Nations International
    Covenant on Economic,
    Social, and Cultural Rights,
    63
United Nations Special
    Rapporteur on Torture, 63
United States (U.S.), 160
    aging of, 76
    agriculture in, 129
    apparel industry in, 11
    budget deficits of, 76
    China and, 155
    China investment in, 110–113
    as China trade partner, 17
    as debtor, 94
    economy of, 3, 76
    education in, 10–11
    employment in, 76
    exports of, 89
    health care in, 10–11
    income gap in, 77
    incomes in, 10
    Japan and, 76
    market of, 13
    military of, 13–14

North Korea and, 145
    oil and, 112
    population of, 76
    protectionism in, 12
    savings in, 28
    Taiwan and, 123, 127
    trade controls by, 11
    trade deficit of, 78, 79, 90, 91
Unocal, 75, 110, 112, 130
Urbanization, 31–32, 46
U.S. *See* United States
U.S. bonds, 108
U.S. Bureau of the Census, 100,
    104
U.S.-China Senior Dialogue,
    123, 160
U.S. Commission on
    International Religious
    Freedom, 65
U.S. Congressional-Executive
    Commission on China, 64
U.S. Department of Commerce,
    80
U.S. Department of Defense,
    136, 180
U.S. Department of State, 63
U.S. Department of Treasury,
    110
U.S. Trade Representative, 97
Uzbekistan, 126, 131

Venezuela, 132
Venture capital, 107
Video games, 96
Vietnam, 115
Voice of America, 65

Wages, 74, 79, 87–89
Wal-Mart, 11, 81
Wars
  Iraq, 141, 149
  Korean, 146
  Sino-Japanese, 119
Water, 54–55
Weapons
  China and, 134
  nuclear, 123, 145, 147, 148
  proliferation of, 1
  Russia and, 134
  trafficking in, 9, 157
Wen Jiabao, 43, 57, 58, 63
WHO. *See* World Health
  Organization
Wolf, Martin, 24
World Bank, 56, 87, 104, 115,
  163, 174
World Health Organization
  (WHO), 51, 54

World Intellectual Property
  Organization (WIPO), 98
World Trade Organization
  (WTO), 11, 22, 36, 67, 84,
  95, 98, 114, 115, 129
WTO. *See* World Trade
  Organization
Wu Bangguo, 57
Wu Guanzheng, 57

Xinjiang, 119, 120, 134

Yasukuni shrine, 142, 144

Zeng Qinghong, 57
Zhou Enlai, 177
Zimbabwe, 13, 140–141
Zoellick, Robert, 159, 160

PublicAffairs is a publishing house founded in 1997. It is a tribute to the standards, values, and flair of three persons who have served as mentors to countless reporters, writers, editors, and book people of all kinds, including me.

I.F. STONE, proprietor of *I. F. Stone's Weekly*, combined a commitment to the First Amendment with entrepreneurial zeal and reporting skill and became one of the great independent journalists in American history. At the age of eighty, Izzy published *The Trial of Socrates*, which was a national bestseller. He wrote the book after he taught himself ancient Greek.

BENJAMIN C. BRADLEE was for nearly thirty years the charismatic editorial leader of *The Washington Post*. It was Ben who gave the *Post* the range and courage to pursue such historic issues as Watergate. He supported his reporters with a tenacity that made them fearless and it is no accident that so many became authors of influential, best-selling books.

ROBERT L. BERNSTEIN, the chief executive of Random House for more than a quarter century, guided one of the nation's premier publishing houses. Bob was personally responsible for many books of political dissent and argument that challenged tyranny around the globe. He is also the founder and longtime chair of Human Rights Watch, one of the most respected human rights organizations in the world.

For fifty years, the banner of PublicAffairs Press was carried by its owner Morris B. Schnapper, who published Gandhi, Nasser, Toynbee, Truman, and about 1,500 other authors. In 1983, Schnapper was described by *The Washington Post* as "a redoubtable gadfly." His legacy will endure in the books to come.

Peter Osnos, *Founder and Editor-at-Large*